Contents

100 IRISH LIVES

Martin Wallace

DAVID & CHARLES
Newton Abbot London
BARNES & NOBLE BOOKS
Totowa, New Jersey

For Valerie

British Library Cataloguing in Publication Data

Wallace, Martin
100 Irish lives.
1. Ireland – History – Biography
I. Title
941.5'092'2 DA916
ISBN 0-7153-8331-0

Library of Congress Cataloging in Publication Data

Wallace, Martin
100 Irish lives
1. Ireland – Biography. 2. Historic sites – Ireland – Guide-books. 3. Ireland – Description and travel – 1981 – Guide-books. I. Title. II. Title: One hundred Irish lives.
CT863.W34 1983 914.15'04824 82-24289
ISBN 0-389-20364-5

First published in the USA 1983 by
Barnes & Noble Books
81 Adams Drive
Totowa, New Jersey, 07512

Filmset in Monophoto Ehrhardt by
Latimer Trend & Company Ltd, Plymouth
and printed in Great Britain
by Redwood Burn Ltd, Trowbridge, Wiltshire
for David & Charles (Publishers) Limited
Brunel House Newton Abbot Devon

Introduction

What do I mean by '100 Irish lives'? For a start, I actually mean 101 lives, for I have counted as one life the cousins Somerville and Ross, inseparable even after death. And what is Irish? Most of the men and women in this book were born in Ireland and spent most of their lives there, but I have included a few like James Gandon and Charles Bianconi who, while they were not born in Ireland and claimed no Irish ancestry, made their homes and their distinctive mark there. St Patrick, of course, is one of their number. I have also included several who, like Richard Brinsley Sheridan and George Bernard Shaw, largely lived and achieved their fame outside the island of their birth.

They are a disparate lot, and some are much better known than others. I confess to a particular regard for the Anglo-Irish; for all their faults, a company which includes Jonathan Swift, Edmund Burke and Charles Stewart Parnell merits W. B. Yeats' tag as 'one of the great stocks of Europe'. Alas, the time is long past when a Swift or a Burke could soar to political and intellectual eminence in London; their modern counterparts, blarneying Irish rather than Anglo-Irish, are more likely to be disc jockeys or hosting chat shows. Among the native Irish patriots and statesmen, I admire most such pragmatists as Daniel O'Connell, Michael Collins and more recently Sean Lemass. I also warm to industrious scholars such as George Petrie and John O'Donovan, who helped to preserve Irish music, language, mythology and folklore, and to reawaken a proud interest in Ireland's past. Naturally, I have included many writers, for Ireland's contribution to world literature has been phenomenal; this is perhaps how a small country can best impose its presence on the international stage. There are also a few rogues and vagabonds, for no impression of Ireland would be complete without them.

Within my 100 lives, I see few common characteristics, save that most were good talkers and many lived and (like Oscar Wilde) died beyond their means, whether they began rich or poor. Not a few were naturally combative, ready for physical or verbal conflict, sometimes too quick to take offence. Not a few were driven by a vision, whether of Ireland's political destiny or of such practical matters as efficient farming or legible handwriting. All, I think, loved their country and hoped to see it prosper.

The lives are arranged chronologically, by date of birth. The book is also a guidebook, to be carried with you. As a footnote to many of the lives, I have noted things and places to see and visit. Dr Samuel Johnson once said that the Giant's Causeway in Co Antrim was worth seeing, but not worth going to see. **Visit**, in my footnotes, is a recommendation to go and see, and to be prepared to spend some time there. **See** may indicate nothing more than a statue or the exterior of a house, worth looking at if you are in the neighbourhood but perhaps not more inviting than that. Remember that opening times etc may have changed since this book was prepared, so it would be wise to check before you set out.

Dublin, of course, has many associations with the people in this book, and one of the five maps will help you wander purposefully through the city. The lives are numbered 1–100, and the numbers on the maps refer to these. Consult the maps as you travel through Ireland, and you will travel with an informed eye. I have included some of the local museums particularly associated with my 100 lives, but many more flourish and are usually worth a visit, as are local libraries, bookshops and tourist information offices. Major institutions such as the National Gallery (many of its older paintings are at Malahide Castle, Co Dublin), the National Library and the National Museum in Dublin, and the Ulster Museum in Belfast, scarcely need my recommendation.

Among my notes, you will also find some recommendations for further reading. It is not an exhaustive bibliography and, with a few exceptions, I have concentrated on books published or republished in recent years. Many are paperbacks; where I have cited an original hardback, there is often a paperback edition. Most of the books have bibliographies which will lead you to further reading, if a particular life has whetted your appetite. I should add that the *Dictionary of National Biography* (Oxford University Press) and Henry Boylan's *A Dictionary of Irish Biography* (Gill & Macmillan, Dublin, 1978) provide interesting introductions to more Irish lives than I have been able to include, while John Cowell's *Where they lived in Dublin* (O'Brien Press, Dublin, 1980) is a mine of information.

Four final points. First, I have appended a list of dates in Irish history, to provide some historical context for the biographies. Second, among the great variations in the spelling of names, particularly in the Irish language, I have generally opted for what seems the commonest usage. Third, an apology for any errors; since I have found errors or inconsistencies in many of the books I have consulted, I see no reason why I should be immune, but I have sometimes indicated where there is conflicting evidence. Fourth and most important, this book was written for pleasure, and is meant to be read for pleasure. There is some laughter in it, I hope, and I may occasionally have taken the advice given in a film directed by the Irish American John Ford: 'When the legend becomes fact, print the legend.'

ACKNOWLEDGEMENTS

The illustrations are courtesy of the following:

The National Gallery of Ireland: 2, 3, 8, 9, 13, 14, 15, 17, 21, 22, 27, 28 and 30 (Portraits 8, 9, 13 and 15 are at Malahide Castle, Co Dublin; 22 is at St Enda's, Rathfarnham, Dublin)

Bord Fáilte, Irish Tourist Board: 1, 4, 5, 6, 7, 10, 12, 16, 18, 19, 23, 25, 26, 29 and 31

The Commissioners of Public Works, Ireland: 11

The Ulster Museum, Belfast: 20 and 24

The maps on pages 12–16 are based on the Ordnance Survey by permission of the Government of the Republic of Ireland (Permit No 3948).

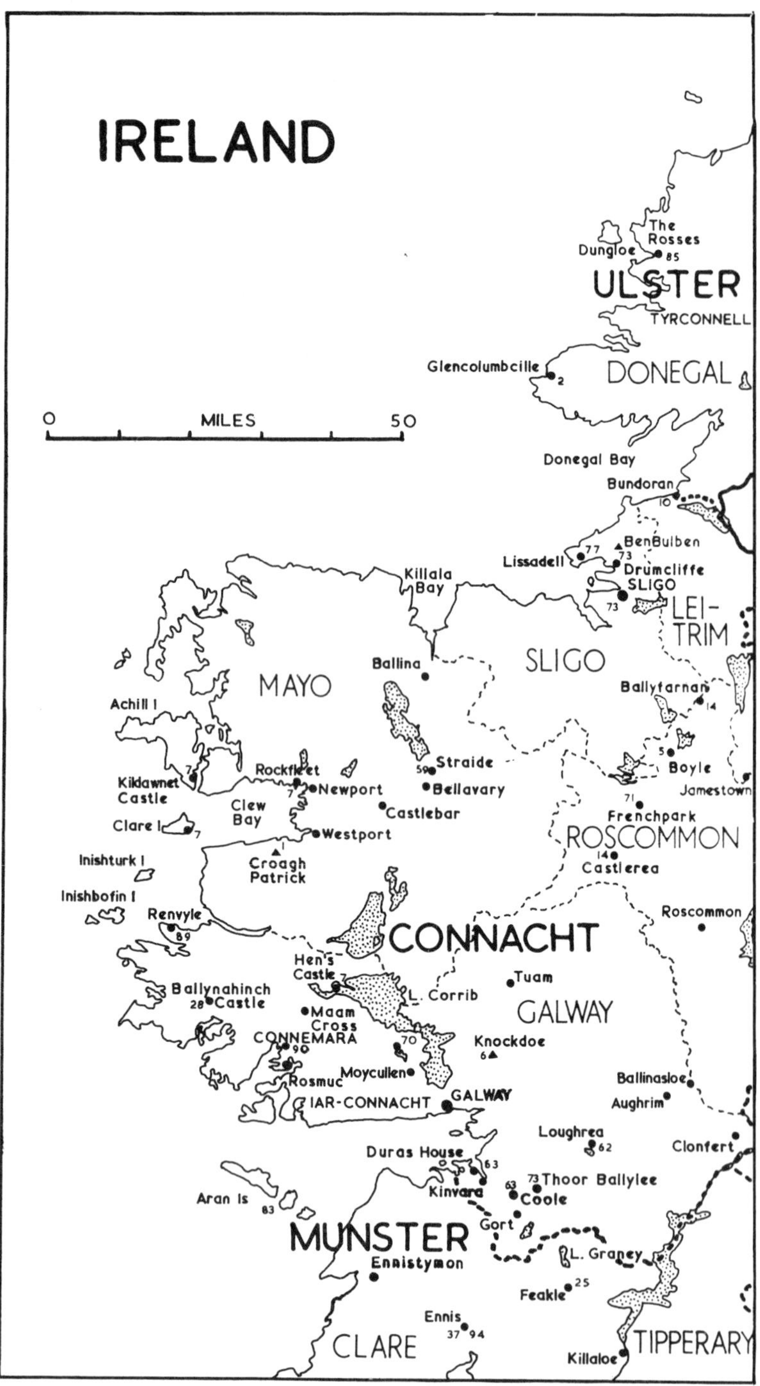
IRELAND
0
MILES
50
The Rosses
Dungloe
85
ULSTER
TYRCONNELL
Glencolumbcille
2
DONEGAL
Donegal Bay
Bundoran
10
Ben Bulben
77
73
Lissadell
Drumcliffe
SLIGO
73
LEI-
TRIM
Killala
Bay
Ballina
SLIGO
MAYO
Ballyfarnan
14
Achill I
Straide
59
Bellavary
5
Boyle
Jamestown
Kildawnet
Castle
7
Rockfleet
7
Newport
Clew
Bay
Castlebar
71
Frenchpark
Clare I
7
Westport
1
Croagh
Patrick
ROSCOMMON
14
Castlerea
Inishturk I
Inishbofin I
Renvyle
89
Roscommon
CONNACHT
Hen's
Castle
7
Tuam
L. Corrib
Ballynahinch
28
Castle
GALWAY
Maam
Cross
CONNEMARA
90
70
Knockdoe
6
Moycullen
Rosmuc
Ballinasloe
IAR-CONNACHT
GALWAY
Aughrim
Loughrea
62
Clonfert
Duras House
63
63
73
Thoor Ballylee
Kinvara
Coole
Aran Is
83
MUNSTER
Gort
L. Graney
Ennistymon
25
Feakle
Ennis
37
94
CLARE
Killaloe
TIPPERARY

Map 1

L. Swilly
DONEGAL
Magilligan
Downhill
Castlerock
Murlough Bay
Ballycastle
Lisboy
Ballymoney
ANTRIM
Drum Ceatt
Gartan
LONDONDERRY
Camnish
Dungiven
LONDONDERRY
Glenarm
Letterkenny
Raphoe
Slemish
Grillagh
Maghera
Duneane
Stranorlar
Ballybofey
Strabane
L. Beg
Randalstown
Carrickfergus
Kilroot
TYRONE
Donegore
Bangor
Cookstown
Lough Neagh
BELFAST
Conlig
Movilla
L. Derg
ULSTER
Newtownards
Pettigo
Dungannon
Moira
Hillsborough
L. Erne
Blackwatertown
Lurgan
Prillisk
Springtown
Portadown
Growell
Killyleagh
Clogher
Benburb
Yellow Ford
Enniskillen
Banbridge
Saul
Lisgoole
ARMAGH
Downpatrick
Glaslough
Cleenish
ARMAGH
DOWN
FERMANAGH
Ballykinler
Clontibret
Newry
Newbliss
MONAGHAN
BREIFNE
LEITRIM
Cloughoughter Castle
Inniskeen
DUNDALK
Mohill
CAVAN
Battle of the Boyne
Nobber
LOUTH
Monasterboice
LONGFORD
Oldcastle
Mellifont Abbey
Edgeworthstown
Loughcrew
Kells
Slane
DROGHEDA
Ardagh
Tailte
Lanesborough
Navan
Tara
L. Ree
Pallas
Trim
DUBLIN
Ballymahon
WESTMEATH
Dunsany Castle
Laracor
Drumcondra
Lissoy
Clonard
MEATH
Clontarf
Killinure
Howth
Athlone
Leixlip
Dunsink
Clonskeagh
Kilbeggan
Maynooth
DUBLIN
Blackrock
Celbridge
Clongowes Wood
Rathmines
Dun Laoghaire
Durrow Abbey
Dalkey
Newcastle
Sandycove
Tullamore
Bodenstown
Ballaly
Kill
Monkstown
OFFALY
KILDARE
Ballybrack
Rathfarnham
Tinnehinch
Foxrock
Greystones
Dundrum
Portarlington
Birr
LEINSTER
WICKLOW
Ballitore
Annamoe
Athy
LAOIS
Moone
Rathdrum
Abbeyleix
Avondale
TIPPERARY
KILKENNY
CARLOW

Map 2

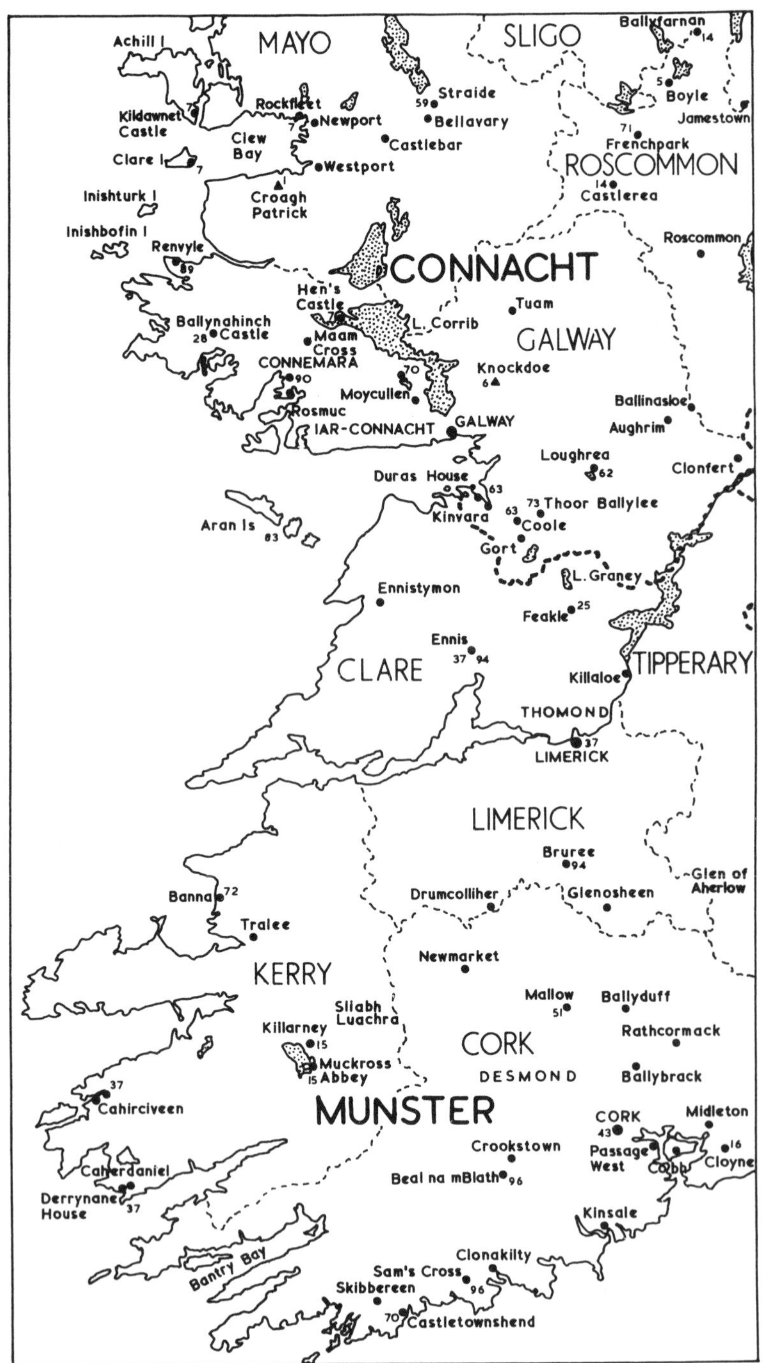

MAYO
SLIGO
Achill I
Ballyfarnan
14
Straide
59
Bellavary
5
Boyle
Jamestown
Kildawnet Castle
7
Rockfleet
7
Newport
Castlebar
Clew Bay
71
Frenchpark
Clare I
7
Westport
ROSCOMMON
14
Castlerea
1
Croagh Patrick
Inishturk I
Inishbofin I
Renvyle
89
Roscommon
CONNACHT
Hen's Castle
70
Tuam
Ballynahinch Castle
28
L. Corrib
GALWAY
Maam Cross
CONNEMARA
90
70
Knockdoe
6
Moycullen
Rosmuc
Ballinasloe
Aughrim
IAR-CONNACHT
GALWAY
Loughrea
62
Clonfert
Duras House
63
63
73
Thoor Ballylee
Kinvara
Coole
Aran Is
83
Gort
L. Graney
Ennistymon
Feakle
25
Ennis
37
94
CLARE
TIPPERARY
Killaloe
THOMOND
37
LIMERICK
LIMERICK
Bruree
94
Glen of Aherlow
Banna
72
Drumcolliher
Glenosheen
Tralee
Newmarket
KERRY
Mallow
51
Ballyduff
Sliabh Luachra
Killarney
15
Rathcormack
CORK
Muckross Abbey
15
DESMOND
Ballybrack
37
Cahirciveen
MUNSTER
CORK
43
Midleton
Crookstown
Passage West
Cobh
16
Cloyne
Caherdaniel
Beal na mBlath
96
Derrynane House
37
Kinsale
Bantry Bay
Clonakilty
Sam's Cross
96
Skibbereen
70
Castletownshend

Map 3

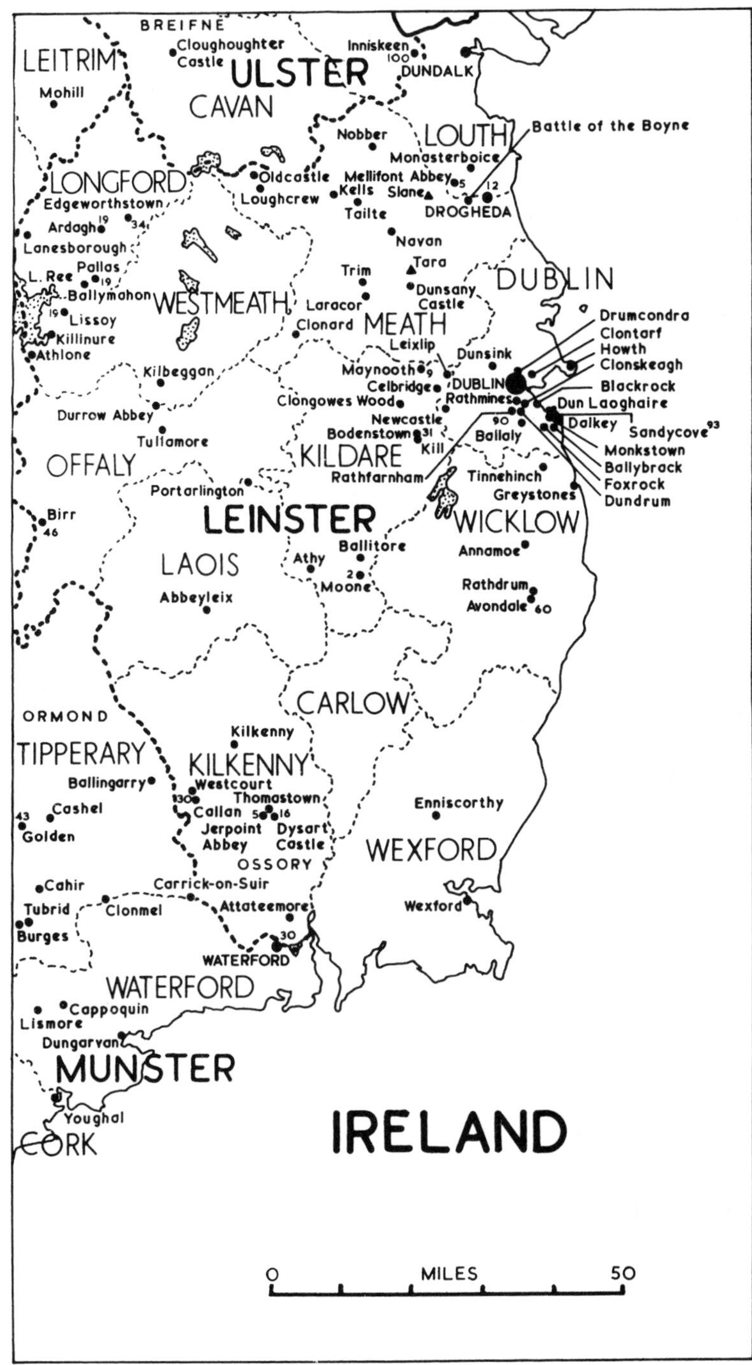

BREIFNE
LEITRIM
Cloughoughter Castle
ULSTER
Inniskeen
100
DUNDALK
Mohill
CAVAN
Nobber
LOUTH
Battle of the Boyne
Monasterboice
LONGFORD
Oldcastle
Mellifont Abbey
5
12
Loughcrew
Kells
Slane
Edgeworthstown
Tailte
DROGHEDA
Ardagh
19
34
Navan
Lanesborough
Tara
Pallas
Trim
L. Ree
19
DUBLIN
Ballymahon
WESTMEATH
Dunsany Castle
19
Lissoy
Laracor
Drumcondra
Killinure
Clonard
MEATH
Clontarf
Athlone
Leixlip
Howth
Dunsink
Clonskeagh
Kilbeggan
Maynooth
9
Celbridge
DUBLIN
Blackrock
Clongowes Wood
Rathmines
Dun Laoghaire
Durrow Abbey
Newcastle
90
Dalkey
Bodenstown
31
Sandycove
93
Tullamore
Ballaly
Kill
Monkstown
OFFALY
KILDARE
Ballybrack
Rathfarnham
Tinnehinch
Foxrock
Portarlington
Greystones
Dundrum
Birr
46
LEINSTER
WICKLOW
Ballitore
Annamoe
LAOIS
Athy
2
Moone
Rathdrum
Abbeyleix
Avondale
60
CARLOW
ORMOND
Kilkenny
TIPPERARY
KILKENNY
Ballingarry
Westcourt
Thomastown
130
Enniscorthy
Cashel
Callan
5
16
43
Golden
Jerpoint Abbey
Dysart Castle
WEXFORD
OSSORY
Cahir
Carrick-on-Suir
Tubrid
Clonmel
Attateemore
Wexford
Burges
30
WATERFORD
WATERFORD
Cappoquin
Lismore
Dungarvan
MUNSTER
Youghal
IRELAND
CORK
0
MILES
50

Map 4

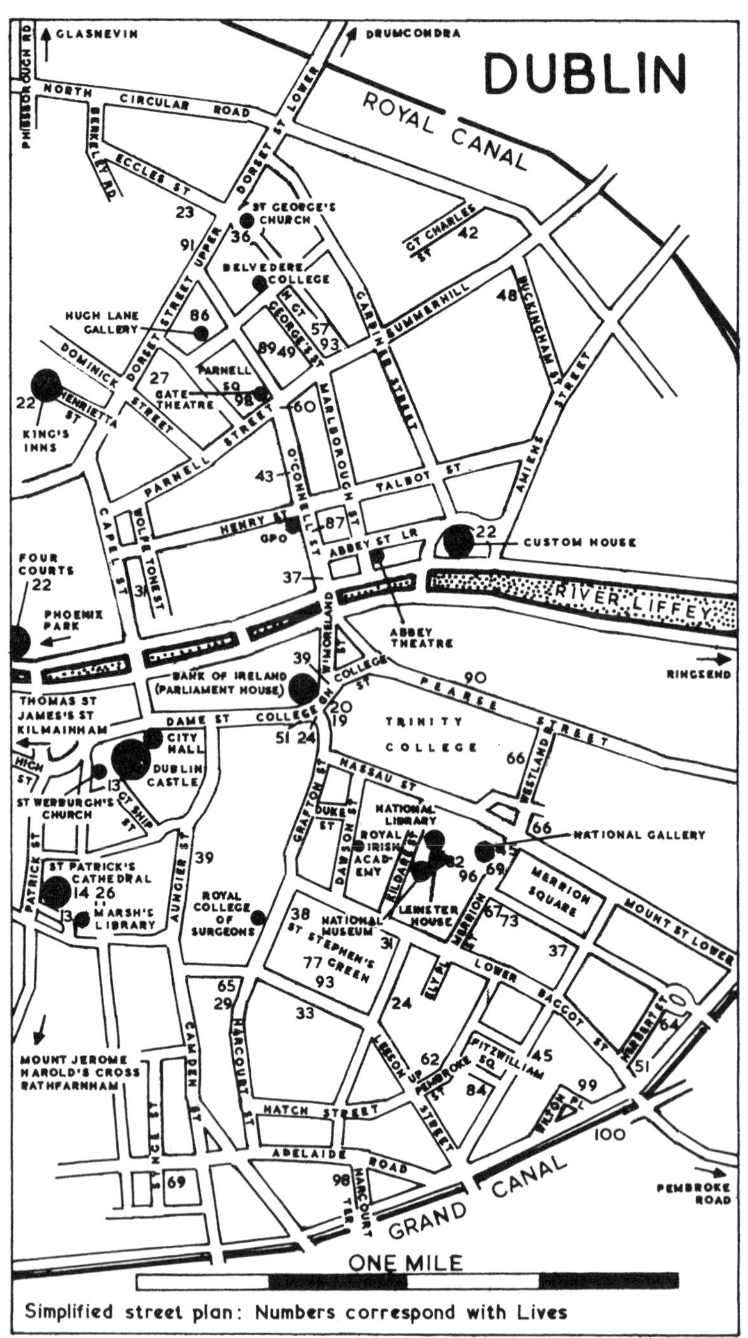
DUBLIN
GLASNEVIN
DRUMCONDRA
ROYAL CANAL
NORTH CIRCULAR ROAD
PHIBSBOROUGH RD
BERKELEY RD
ECCLES ST
DORSET ST LOWER
ST GEORGE'S CHURCH
BELVEDERE COLLEGE
GT CHARLES ST
SUMMERHILL
BUCKINGHAM ST
HUGH LANE GALLERY
DORSET STREET UPPER
N GT GEORGE'S ST
GARDINER STREET
DOMINICK STREET
HENRIETTA ST
KING'S INNS
PARNELL SQ
GATE THEATRE
PARNELL STREET
MARLBOROUGH ST
O'CONNELL ST
TALBOT ST
AMIENS STREET
CAPEL ST
WOLFE TONE ST
HENRY ST
GPO
ABBEY ST LR
CUSTOM HOUSE
FOUR COURTS
PHOENIX PARK
RIVER LIFFEY
ABBEY THEATRE
WESTMORELAND ST
BANK OF IRELAND (PARLIAMENT HOUSE)
COLLEGE GN
COLLEGE ST
PEARSE STREET
RINGSEND
THOMAS ST
JAMES'S ST
KILMAINHAM
DAME ST
CITY HALL
DUBLIN CASTLE
TRINITY COLLEGE
HIGH ST
ST WERBURGH'S CHURCH
GT SHIP ST
NASSAU ST
GRAFTON ST
DUKE ST
DAWSON ST
NATIONAL LIBRARY
ROYAL IRISH ACADEMY
KILDARE ST
WESTLAND RO
NATIONAL GALLERY
MERRION SQUARE
ST PATRICK'S CATHEDRAL
PATRICK ST
AUNGIER ST
MARSH'S LIBRARY
ROYAL COLLEGE OF SURGEONS
NATIONAL MUSEUM
LEINSTER HOUSE
MERRION ST
ST STEPHEN'S GREEN
MOUNT ST LOWER
LOWER BAGGOT ST
ELY PL
HERBERT ST
LEESON ST UP
PEMBROKE ST
FITZWILLIAM SQ
UPTON PL
CAMDEN ST
HARCOURT ST
MOUNT JEROME
HAROLD'S CROSS
RATHFARNHAM
HATCH STREET
ADELAIDE ROAD
HARCOURT TER
GRAND CANAL
PEMBROKE ROAD
ONE MILE
Simplified street plan: Numbers correspond with Lives

Map 5

—I—

SAINT PATRICK

c390–c461

APOSTLE OF IRELAND

Precise dates cannot be attached to St Patrick's life, and modern scholars differ as much as the compilers of ancient Irish annals have done. Of the writings attributed to him, only his *Confession* and *Letter to Coroticus* are confidently accepted as his work, and they are uninformative. In one theory, there may even have been two Patricks. Ireland's patron saint was probably born towards the end of the fourth century; his father, Calpornius, was a minor functionary in Roman Britain. At sixteen, Patrick was captured by Irish raiders and apparently sold to a chieftain, Milchu, whose animals he herded on Slemish mountain, Co Antrim. Six years later, he escaped to southern Ireland and sailed aboard a ship carrying a cargo of wolfhounds, possibly to France.

In captivity, Patrick had turned to God, and in dreams had been told to escape; later, he was to have a vision in which the people of Ireland called him to walk among them again. One tradition suggests that Patrick became a disciple of Germanus at Auxerre, in France, and that he set out to convert the Irish after the death of Palladius, whom the Pope had sent to Ireland in 431. Certainly, his arrival as bishop is commonly dated at 432, his first church being a barn donated by Dichu, a local chief, at Saul, Co Down (*sabhall* being the Irish word for 'barn').

Eventually, he made his headquarters at Armagh, which has remained the ecclesiastical capital of Ireland. He travelled widely, baptising converts, ordaining bishops and fostering the monastic life which characterised the Irish Church. He was proud of his Roman citizenship, but his early captivity had usefully equipped him to preach to the Irish in their native tongue. His sense of mission was overwhelming, and he was unconcerned about personal safety or comfort in challenging the prevailing druidical paganism.

There are many legends about St Patrick: that he banished snakes from Ireland; that he used the three-leaved shamrock to demonstrate the Holy Trinity; that he lit a Paschal fire on the Hill of

Slane, Co Meath, challenging the pagan flame on nearby Tara. Such stories helped the early chroniclers turn a bishop of the Church, possibly one of several contemporary missionaries, into a symbolic figure. What is not in doubt is that Patrick helped the Roman Church conquer Ireland as the Roman Empire had never done.

Irish annals generally date Patrick's death at 493, but an earlier date of 461 is also recorded, which fits better with Palladius' known death. He is commonly believed to have died at Saul and been buried at Downpatrick, Co Down. As to the actual day of his death, 17 March is celebrated throughout the world as St Patrick's Day.

Visit Croagh Patrick, Co Mayo (6 miles/9.5 km WSW of Westport), where Patrick spent forty days of Lent, attracts thousands of Catholic pilgrims on the last Sunday in July. Lough Derg, Co Donegal (5 miles/8 km N of Pettigo), similarly attracts pilgrims (a three-day programme, 1 June–15 Aug).
See At Saul, the Church of Ireland has built a replica of an early Christian church and round tower. At St Patrick's Cathedral, Downpatrick, a granite block marks the supposed (but unlikely) grave of SS Patrick, Brigid and Colmcille.
Read Joseph Duffy, *Patrick in his own words* (Veritas, Dublin, 1975) largely presents the saint as revealed by the saint's own *Confession.*

—2—

SAINT COLMCILLE

521–597
'DOVE OF THE CHURCH'

St Colmcille was born on 7 December 521 in Gartan, Co Donegal. On the same day, according to legend, the dying St Buite, founder of Monasterboice monastery in Co Louth, foretold the imminent birth of 'a child illustrious before God'. His father Fedhlimidh was a great grandson of Niall of the Nine Hostages, the high king and forebear of the Ulster O'Neills, and his mother Eithne was descended from Cathair Mor, King of Leinster. He was baptised

Colm or Colum (and is also known as Columba, the Latin 'dove', though his nature was far from pacific), *cille* ('of the church') being added later.

As a chief's son, he was fostered out – but, unusually, to a priest – and later studied at the monastic schools of Moville Abbey, Co Down, and Clonard, Co Meath, as well as acquiring poetic skills from a Leinster bard named Gemman. His seventh-century biographer, St Adomnán, describes him praying successfully at Moville for spring water to be turned into communion wine; later writers also ascribed many miracles to him. The episcopal church which St Patrick (*qv*) had founded gradually evolved into one dominated by monastic settlements, and Colmcille returned to his native Ulster to found his first monastery at Derry in 546. Thereafter, he travelled throughout Ireland, establishing many new settlements; the most notable was Durrow Abbey in Co Offaly, renowned for its scholarship and illuminated manuscripts.

In 563, Colmcille and twelve followers sailed to the Scottish island of Iona, and founded a monastery which remained the inspiration of Celtic Christianity until the Viking raids of the eighth century. According to tradition, Colmcille had secretly copied a psalter belonging to St Finnian of Moville; Finnian discovered this and claimed the copy. In an early copyright adjudication, the high king Diarmuid ruled 'To every cow her calf, and to every book its copy.' Diarmuid also angered Colmcille by killing a youth to whom the priest had given sanctuary, and the imperious Colmcille persuaded his Uí Néill kinsmen to wage war on the high king. The Uí Néill were victorious in the battle of Cuildreimhne, at the foot of Ben Bulben, Co Sligo, in 561, but Colmcille was shocked by the numbers slain. After a synod of saints at Tailte, Co Meath, had charged him to convert as many pagans as there were dead men at Cuildreimhne, Colmcille chose exile to work among the Pictish tribes of Scotland.

Colmcille was statesman and prince as well as churchman, and as well as establishing many Scottish monasteries he was influential in the growth of the Scottish kingdom of Dalriada. In 575 he helped to establish its virtual independence from Irish Dalriada at a convention held at Drum Ceatt, Co Londonderry. At the same time he is believed to have persuaded King Aedh not to banish the bards or *filidh*, who had abused their privileged position; in future, these itinerant poets were to moderate their satires and make fewer demands on those who gave them hospitality. St Colmcille died in Iona on 9 June 597.

Visit Columban sites at Durrow Abbey (4½ miles/7 km NE of Tullamore, Co Offaly), remains include a fine tenth-century high cross; Moone (2½ miles/4km S of Ballitore, Co Kildare), with slender ninth-century high cross; Glencolumbcille, Co Donegal, where each 9 June a 3-mile/4.5 km *turas* or pilgrimage embraces fifteen 'stations' associated with the saint.
See The *Cathach*, a sixth/seventh-century psalter possibly written by the saint, preserved at the Royal Irish Academy, 19 Dawson St, Dublin; the seventh-century Book of Durrow and the eighth-century Book of Kells (from a Columban monastery in Co Meath), both in Trinity College, Dublin.
Read Ian Finlay, *Columba* (Gollancz, 1979), a shrewd examination of the elusive evidence concerning the saint's life and times.

—3— SAINT COLUMBANUS

*c*543–615 THE FIRST EUROPEAN

Little is reliably known of Columbanus' early life, and there are inconsistencies in the seventh-century biography by Jonas of Susa, but he was probably born *c*543 in Leinster. He left home as a youth to study at Cleenish, Co Fermanagh, and then entered the monastery at Bangor, Co Down, founded by St Comgall. In time, he felt a call to missionary work abroad, and *c*589 he and twelve followers sailed for Europe.

He is thought to have landed in France near St Malo, and after preaching in the region he was summoned to the court of the Frankish king of Burgundy, Gunthram or possibly Childebert II. Columbanus was allowed to settle in the mountainous wilderness of the Vosges, and he built a monastery at Anegray. According to legend, Columbanus found his own retreat in a bear's den; a holy well marks where he brought water from the barren rock. A second monastery was soon necessary at nearby Luxeuil, and it became famous for scholarship. When a third was opened at Fontaine, Columbanus drew up his *Regula Monachorum*, a strict code emphasising obedience 'even unto death', poverty and mortification through fasting as requirements of monastic life.

There were differences in practice between the Celtic and Roman Churches – as in the dating of Easter, the Irish practice of private confession and penance, even the manner of shaving a monk's head – and Columbanus came into conflict with local bishops. In time, his outspokenness lost him favour at court, and in 610 the Irish monks were expelled by Theuderich II, finally reaching Nantes some six hundred miles away. He was prepared to return to Ireland, but storms persuaded both the elderly saint and his enemies that it was God's intention that he remain.

Eventually, Columbanus reached Metz, where King Theudebert invited him to preach to the pagan tribes of central Europe. He settled at Bregenz, on the shore of Lake Constance, but when the king was defeated by Theuderich in 612, Columbanus was forced to move to Lombardy. King Agilulf offered him land at Bobbio, in the Apennines, and he built a new monastery. He died there on 23 November 615, having sent a deathbed message of forgiveness to his last Irish companion, Gall, who had refused to leave Lake Constance. St Gall, it transpired, had already celebrated mass for Columbanus, having learned of his death in a vision.

Columbanus has been described as Ireland's first European, and many followed in his footsteps. The French statesman, Robert Schuman, dubbed him the patron saint of those who seek to construct a united Europe.

Read Tomás Ó Fiach, *Columbanus in his own words* (Veritas, Dublin, 1974) is a readable biography, including translations of the saint's rules, letters, sermons and poetry.

—4—
BRIAN BORU
*c*940–1014
HIGH KING

Brian was born *c*940 in north Munster, the youngest son of Cennétig, king of the Dál Cais. In 976, he succeeded his murdered brother Mahon or Mathgamain, and claimed the kingship of Munster; in 978, he slew his rival for the crown, Maelmuad of the Eóganacht. The two brothers had already won some victories over the Vikings or Norsemen, who since 800 had founded ports at Dublin, Wexford, Waterford, Cork and Limerick. The Norse longboats easily penetrated Munster, and Brian was the first Irish ruler to assemble a fleet to defend and extend his territory.

By 984, Brian had extended his rule eastward over Ossory and Leinster. His principal Irish rival was now Malachy, king of Meath, who had become high king at Tara in 980. Malachy had defeated a Norse army at Tara and driven the Viking Olaf out of Dublin; Olaf's son, Sitric, eventually ruled Dublin under Malachy. Brian's seat was at Kincora (now Killaloe, Co Clare), near Lough Derg, and he was able to sail up the river Shannon to ravage Connacht, Meath and Breifne. In 997, after much fighting, the two kings met near Clonfert, Co Galway, and agreed to divide Ireland between them, Brian gaining suzerainty over Dublin. In 999, the Leinstermen joined with Sitric against Brian, only to suffer defeat at Glenmama, Co Wicklow.

Brian married Gormflath (who had been married successively to Olaf and Malachy), gave his own daughter to Sitric, and claimed the northern half of Ireland. Malachy failed to marshal the support of the Northern Uí Néill, and in 1002 conceded the high kingship. Collecting tribute and hostages on his royal journeys, Brian now acquired the name Boru (Brian of the Tributes), but the extent of his authority was probably exaggerated by later chroniclers. He visited Armagh in 1005, donating twenty ounces of gold to the Church and recognising the archbishop as primate of all Ireland.

In 1013, the unfaithful Gormflath roused Sitric and her brother

Maelmora, king of Leinster, against Malachy. Brian came to Malachy's aid, but failed to take Dublin and retired to Kincora. Sitric made an alliance with Sigurd, earl of Orkney, who delivered 2,000 Norse soldiers and was promised Gormflath in marriage. A new battle was joined at Clontarf, outside Dublin, on Good Friday, 23 April 1014. The Leinstermen and Vikings were finally routed, but the aged Brian was slain in his tent. The Vikings were no longer a military threat, but Brian's death foreshadowed new dynastic conflicts which left Ireland vulnerable to the Norman invasion in 1169.

See A tablet in the outer wall of the north transept of Armagh Cathedral marks Brian's reputed grave.
Read Morgan Llywelyn, *Lion of Ireland: The Legend of Brian Boru* (Bodley Head, 1980), a lively novel.

—5—
SAINT MALACHY
1094–1148
CHURCH REFORMER

Malachy's full name was Mael M'Aodhog Ua Morgair. He was the son of a renowned teacher in Armagh, and he was probably born there in 1094. A devout and studious boy, Malachy attached himself to a hermit, Imar, and so impressed the bishop of Armagh, Cellach, that he made him his vicar. He was ordained in 1119, and soon showed a reforming zeal in establishing the Roman liturgy and in such matters as confession, confirmation and marriage rites.

The Celtic Church had largely lost its early ascetic tradition, and abuses were prevalent. In the monasteries, the post of abbot was often handed down within a family; some abbots were laymen, some were married. Within the Church, reformers saw the need to enforce higher standards through a strong central organisation wielding authority derived from Rome. In 1121, Malachy went to Lismore monastery, Co Waterford, to study under Malchus, a bishop knowledgeable about the Church in England and Rome.

In 1123, he became abbot of Bangor, Co Down, rebuilding the

monastery which Vikings had destroyed, and in 1124 bishop of Down and Connor. In 1129, the dying Cellach named Malachy as his successor, breaking the hereditary tradition in the primatial see. A usurper claimed the bishopric, and Malachy was not consecrated until 1132; nor did he enter the city of Armagh until 1134. Having restored peace and discipline, he resigned to return to Down in 1137, founding an Augustinian priory at Downpatrick, Co Down.

Malachy clearly remained influential, for in 1139 he set out for Rome to seek from the Pope the symbolic pallium or lambswool collar for the archbishops of Armagh and Cashel. On his journey, he stayed at the abbey of Clairvaux, in north-east France, where he met his future biographer, St Bernard. So impressed was he that, on his return journey, he left four companions to train in the austere Cistercian discipline. In 1142, Mellifont Abbey became the first of thirty-nine Cistercian foundations in Ireland, an incursion which, with other reforms and the Anglo-Norman invasion, signalled the end of the Celtic Church.

Malachy would have remained at Clairvaux, but Pope Innocent II insisted he return to Ireland as papal legate, and convene a council of clergy and kings to make a formal request for the pallia. He was now able diplomatically to continue his reform work, and it was 1148 before he set out again for Rome. In poor health, Malachy died at Clairvaux on 2 November 1148. The great reformer was canonised by Clement III in 1190.

Visit Mellifont Abbey (5 miles/8 km NW of Drogheda, Co Louth), Boyle Abbey, 1148 (Boyle, Co Roscommon), and Jerpoint Abbey, 1180 (1 mile/1.5 km SW of Thomastown, Co Kilkenny) are among the most interesting Cistercian remains.
See A plaque marks the saint's reputed birthplace in Ogle St, Armagh.
Read Brian Scott, *Malachy* (Veritas, Dublin, 1976).

—6—

GARRET MORE FITZGERALD

8th EARL OF KILDARE

*c*1456–1513

THE GREAT EARL

Gerald Fitzgerald, whom the Irish called Garret More, was probably born in Maynooth Castle, Co Kildare, *c*1456. At the time, there were three great Anglo-Irish families. The Geraldines or Fitzgeralds of Leinster (earls of Kildare) and of Munster (earls of Desmond) both supported the House of York in England's Wars of the Roses; the Butlers (earls of Ormond) supported Lancaster. The 7th Earl had lately established Kildare supremacy, and when Garret More succeeded to the title in 1478, he was to secure this pre-eminence for a further half-century.

In the absence of a king's deputy, he was immediately elected as caretaker 'justiciar' by the Irish Council (the deputy's advisers and ministers), and was strong enough to resist King Edward IV's attempt to install an English deputy, Lord Grey. He then sailed to England where he was confirmed as deputy, a post he held intermittently under successive English kings. Through judicious marriage alliances, linking the Old English lords and the Gaelic chiefs, Kildare steadily extended his influence.

In 1485, the Lancastrian Henry VII ascended the English throne; two years later, Kildare accepted a young pretender, Lambert Simnel, as rightful occupant of the throne. Simnel was crowned in Dublin, but an invasion of England failed; however, Kildare was fully pardoned. Another pretender, Perkin Warbeck, landed in Cork in 1491, and Kildare came under suspicion. He was removed from office in 1492, and a new deputy, Edward Poynings, arrived with armed men to restore English sovereignty. Poynings' parliament of 1494–5 accused Kildare of treason, and he was imprisoned in the Tower of London. The so-called Poynings' Law subordinated the hitherto independent Irish parliament to the king.

Kildare was restored as deputy in 1496. He is said to have treated Henry VII as an equal, evoking the king's response: 'Since all Ireland cannot rule this man, this man must rule Ireland.' Certainly, no one else could have preserved peace so well, and the 'Great Earl' held office until his death. In 1504, he defeated his son-in-law, Ulick Burke of Clanrickard, at Knockdoe, Co Galway, and received the Order of the Garter. It was the first Irish battle employing firearms; on 3 September 1513, Kildare himself was killed by a musket during a skirmish with the O'Mores of Laois. The new deputy was his son, Garret Oge, but Poynings' Law already foreshadowed a centralised monarchy, and a second conquest of Ireland would soon mark the end of the Gaelic lordships and the native culture which had flowered under Kildare.

See Remains of Maynooth Castle, at the entrance to St Patrick's College, Maynooth, Co Kildare.

—7— GRACE O'MALLEY

*c*1530–*c*1603 PIRATE QUEEN

Grace O'Malley was born *c*1530 in Co Mayo. Among the many variants of her name, Gráinne Ni Mháille is common; she is also called Granuaile or Gráinne Mhaol (Grace of the cropped hair), having adopted a boy's haircut to sail to Spain on her father's ship. He was Owen 'Black Oak' O'Malley, chieftain of the lands around Clew Bay. The O'Malleys were noted seafarers, engaging in piracy as well as trading and fishing, and Grace spent much of her childhood on such islands as Clare, Inishturk and Inishbofin.

She married Donal O'Flaherty *c*1546. His family ruled Iar-Connacht and Connemara, and she joined readily in her husband's piracy; Galway city's west gate was inscribed 'From the ferocious O'Flaherties good Lord deliver us'. However, as the English administration gradually extended into Connacht, Gaelic chieftains had to submit in return for a regrant of their traditional lands.

Donal is thought to have died in battle with the Joyces after he seized a castle on Lough Corrib; he was known as Donal the Cock, and the fortress was named Hen's Castle after Grace's subsequent spirited defence. For a time, Grace made Clare Island the headquarters of her piracy, but in 1566 she married Richard Burke, whose Rockfleet Castle guarded a safe harbour on the north of Clew Bay. One legend suggests she dissolved the marriage as he returned from a voyage, but held the castle. More probably, she dominated him until his death in 1583; the lord deputy, Sir Henry Sidney, called her 'a notorious woman in all the coasts of Ireland' when the couple submitted to him at Galway in 1577.

Submission did not curb her behaviour, and she was imprisoned more than once in the following years and at one point fled to Ulster. In 1593, she petitioned Queen Elizabeth for 'free liberty during her life to invade with sword and fire all your highness' enemies', and sailed up the Thames to meet the Queen at Greenwich Castle. One legend is that she refused a title, considering herself of equal rank, but her son became 1st Viscount Mayo in 1627. Grace's suit was apparently successful, but the governor of Connacht, Sir Richard Bingham, considered her 'a notable traitress and nurse of all rebellions in the province for forty years' and continued to harass her until he left Connacht in 1595. Of her last years little is known, but her lands were plundered and it is thought she died in poverty *c*1603.

See Well preserved among the many castles associated with Grace O'Malley are Rockfleet (3 miles/4.5 km W of Newport, Co Mayo), Kildawnet Castle on Achill Island, and one on Clare Island. She may be buried in the latter island's abbey, where a stone plaque bears the O'Malley arms and *Terra marique potens* (Powerful by land and sea).

Read Anne Chambers, *Granuaile: The Life and Times of Grace O'Malley* (Wolfhound Press, Portmarnock, Co Dublin, 1979).

—8—
HUGH O'NEILL
2nd EARL OF TYRONE
1550–1616
THE GREAT O'NEILL

O'Neill was born at Dungannon, Co Tyrone, in 1550, entering a Gaelic world of tribal rivalry, passion and intrigue. His father was Matthew O'Neill, 1st Baron Dungannon and illegitimate son of Conn O'Neill, Earl of Tyrone and 'The O'Neill'. Matthew's claim to the earlship was disputed by his half-brother, Shane O'Neill, who procured his murder. When Conn died in 1559 and Shane became The O'Neill, Hugh was taken into the protection of the Queen's deputy, Sir Henry Sidney, and raised as an English nobleman.

In 1567, Shane was succeeded by his son, Turlough. In 1568, Hugh finally settled in Ulster. Initially loyal to Queen Elizabeth, he led a troop of horse against the Desmond rebellion of 1569, and in 1573 assisted the 1st Earl of Essex in an attempted colonisation of Co Antrim. In 1587, O'Neill was formally granted the Earlship of Tyrone, and in 1593 the ailing Turlough ceded the Irish title of The O'Neill.

There had been earlier suspicions about O'Neill's reliability, particularly when he disobeyed government instructions to kill survivors of the 1588 Spanish Armada. However, the enmity between Hugh and Turlough had ensured that neither became too powerful; as The O'Neill, Hugh was able to unite the Irish chiefs in defence of Gaelic life, law and tradition. Shrewdly, he had trained a substantial army by steadily changing the 600 men he was allowed to keep in the Queen's pay.

In 1595, O'Neill destroyed an English fort near the present Blackwatertown, Co Armagh. He then harried an expedition under Sir Henry Bagenal, his brother-in-law, finally defeating it at Clontibret, Co Monaghan. In 1598, following other skirmishes and truces, O'Neill exploited the boggy Ulster terrain to achieve the greatest Irish victory over an English army, when he defeated and slew Bagenal at the Yellow Ford, near Blackwatertown. O'Neill now had many allies, notably the dashing Red Hugh O'Donnell of Tyrconnell, and the English plantation of Munster was quickly swept away.

In 1599, the 2nd Earl of Essex arrived in Ireland with an army, but did no better than negotiate a truce; he was replaced by Lord Mountjoy. O'Neill had long sought aid from Spain, and in 1601 more than 3,000 Spanish soldiers landed at Kinsale, Co Cork, where they were besieged by Mountjoy. O'Neill abandoned his usual caution, marched with O'Donnell to Kinsale, and was routed in a pitched battle. O'Donnell fled to Spain, while O'Neill retreated to Ulster, eventually surrendering in 1603.

Queen Elizabeth had just died, and a friendlier James I restored O'Neill to his earldom, but as a landlord rather than a ruler. Ulster was now subjected to English administration and law, and his Catholic religion was forbidden. In 1607, O'Neill led the 'Flight of the Earls', sailing from Lough Swilly to exile in Europe with more than ninety Gaelic chiefs. He was received with honour in Rome, where he died on 20 July 1616.

Read Seán O'Faoláin, *The Great O'Neill* (Longmans, 1942; Mercier Press, Cork, 1970); G. A. Hayes-McCoy, *Irish Battles* (Longmans, 1969) has chapters on O'Neill's main battles.

—9—
GEOFFREY KEATING
*c*1570–*c*1650
POET AND HISTORIAN

Geoffrey Keating (or Seathrún Céitinn) was born *c*1570 in Burges, Co Tipperary. Of Anglo-Norman stock, he was educated at a local bardic school, and then at Bordeaux, where he studied for the Catholic priesthood. He returned to Ireland *c*1610 as a doctor of theology, and served in different parishes near his birthplace. His popularity as a preacher grew steadily, but after a sermon directed against the mistress of a local squire he had to take refuge in a cave in the Glen of Aherlow.

While in hiding, he began his famous *History of Ireland* or *Foras Feasa ar Éirinn* (literally 'a basis of knowledge about Ireland'), travelling widely to consult manuscripts held in great houses. It was begun in 1629, and completed by the time he emerged as a parish priest in Cappoquin, Co Waterford, in 1634. He returned to Tubrid, near his birthplace, *c*1644 and erected a mortuary chapel in which he was buried. He may have died in that year, but one tradition is that he was murdered in nearby Clonmel by Cromwell's soldiers in 1650.

Keating's major work was the first cohesive history of Ireland written in the Irish language, and it was a counterbalance to the works of English authors such as Edmund Spenser and Giraldus Cambrensis. Copies of the manuscript were widely circulated, and the book remained popular in this form until the middle of the nineteenth century. It was not printed in Irish until the twentieth century, but English translations were published early in the eighteenth century. Keating realised that Gaelic Ireland was disappearing, and his patriotic history helped to preserve the early myths and sagas on which he uncritically drew.

He was also a poet, writing both in the formal bardic style of syllabic verse and in the new stressed verse of the seventeenth century, which was to achieve a wider popularity. Some poems are lyrical; others are patriotic, the new verse proving well suited to impassioned laments for lost heroes and braver times. He also wrote several works of theology, and his *Three Shafts of Death* or *Trí Biorghaoithe an Bháis* is an urbane and scholarly collection of anecdotes, arguments and pieties.

See Keating's vestments are in the museum of St Patrick's College, Maynooth, Co Kildare.

—10—

MÍCHEÁL Ó CLÉIRIGH

c1575–1643
MASTER CHRONICLER

Ó Cléirigh (Michael O'Clery) was born at Kilbarron, overlooking Donegal Bay. His date of birth is commonly given as 1575, but may have been some years later. He was baptised Tadhg, but became Brother Mícheál on entering the Franciscan order at the Irish College of St Antony at Louvain, in Belgium. His family had traditionally been chroniclers for the O'Donnells, and he had already studied Irish history and literature, acquiring a reputation for scholarship.

He spent several years at Louvain before returning in 1626 to Ireland, where he joined the Franciscan convent at Bundrowes, near Bundoran, Co Donegal. His mission was to collect material for a work on the lives of Irish saints, *Acta Sanctorum Hiberniae*, planned by Father Hugh Ward, professor of theology at Louvain, and carried on by Ward's successor, Father John Colgan. Many ancient manuscripts had already been destroyed in the Irish wars; Ó Cléirigh's laboriously compiled copies helped to preserve in Louvain much of the historical record that remained at risk in Ireland. In addition, he began to assemble his own calendar of Irish saints, commonly known as *The Martyrology of Donegal* (1628 and, in an extended version, 1630), in which saints are assigned to their festival days, with accompanying notes on their lives and characters.

Ó Cléirigh next sought the collaboration of three other learned historians, and found a patron in Toirdhealbhach Mac Cochlain. They spent a month at the Franciscan convent of Killinure, Athlone, Co Westmeath, on the shores of Lough Ree, compiling *Réimh Ríoghraidhe na hEireann agus Seanchas na Naomh* (The Succession of the Kings and the Genealogies of the Saints of Ireland). In 1631, the four scholars travelled to the convent of Lisgoole, on the shores of Lough Erne, to begin revising the *Leabhar Gabhála*, the Book of the Invasions of Ireland. Their new patron was Brian Roe Maguire, whose own chronicler joined in the work.

On 22 January 1632, Ó Cléirigh and his three assistants began the *Annála Ríoghachta Éireann* (Annals of the Kingdom of Ireland), which were to become famous as *The Annals of the Four Masters*, a title Colgan used to distinguish this major work from others in the same field. It was completed at Bundrowes on 10 August 1636, under the patronage of Fearghal O Gadhra, and chronicled Irish history from earliest times to the early seventeenth century. The Annals were austerely written, and detailed such major events as wars and raids, the burning and reconstruction of monasteries, the crowning and death of kings; written in Irish, they were translated by John O'Donovan (*qv*) in the nineteenth century. In 1637, Ó Cléirigh returned to Louvain, probably joining Colgan in his work on Irish saints. He also published a glossary of difficult Irish words in 1643, the year in which he died.

Read Brendan Jennings, *Michael O Cleirigh, Chief of the Four Masters, and His Associates* (Talbot Press, Dublin 1936).

—11—

OWEN ROE O'NEILL

*c*1590–1649
PROFESSIONAL SOLDIER

O'Neill's date of birth has traditionally been given as *c*1590, but it may have been several years earlier. His father was Art O'Neill, younger brother of Hugh O'Neill (*qv*). Educated in Spain, O'Neill was commissioned in the newly formed Irish regiment commanded by Henry O'Neill (son of Hugh), and served Spain with distinction for many years. He eventually formed his own regiment, and in 1640 won praise for a gallant defence of Arras; he finally negotiated an honourable surrender to the French commander, who acknowledged that O'Neill had 'surpassed us in all things save good fortune'.

Although a professional soldier, O'Neill was devoted to Ireland and long hoped that Spain would intervene against its Stuart rulers.

When the Irish rebellion of 1641 broke out, O'Neill secured his release from the Spanish army and arrived in Lough Swilly in July 1642. He joined up with Sir Phelim O'Neill, his cousin and instigator of the rebellion, and became general of the Ulster Catholic forces.

The Anglo-Normans or Old English joined the native Irish in the Catholic 'Confederation of Kilkenny', favouring Charles I as his dispute with the English parliament turned into civil war. O'Neill took the confederacy oath in November 1642, receiving supplies for his army to fight the parliamentary army led by the Scottish general, Robert Monro. The Old English always inclined towards a political settlement with the king's deputy, the Earl of Ormond, but the native Irish wanted to uproot the Protestant planters in Ulster and regain confiscated land. O'Neill was encouraged by the papal nuncio, Cardinal Rinuccini, and in 1646 heavily defeated Monro at Benburb, Co Tyrone. It was the first Irish victory in a formal pitched battle.

O'Neill failed to consolidate his success, instead accepting Rinuccini's summons to Kilkenny, where the nuncio rejected a peace offer from Ormond which the Old English favoured. O'Neill abandoned a siege of Dublin after disagreeing with Thomas Preston, the confederacy's inept commander in Leinster; Ormond then surrendered the city to parliamentary forces, which inflicted defeats on Preston and on the confederate army in Munster.

The arrival of Oliver Cromwell in August 1649 persuaded O'Neill to a new defence of his religion; he was the only Irish commander likely to defeat Cromwell. On his way to join a royalist army assembled by Ormond, he died at Cloughoughter Castle in Lough Oughter, Co Cavan, on 6 November 1649.

Read G. A. Hayes-McCoy, *Irish Battles* (Longmans, 1969) includes a chapter on O'Neill and his victory at Benburb.

—12—

SAINT OLIVER PLUNKETT

1625–1681
THE LAST MARTYR

Plunkett (or Plunket) was born on 1 November 1625 at Loughcrew, near Oldcastle, Co Meath. The Plunketts were an influential Anglo-Norman family, and his kinsmen included the Earls of Roscommon and Fingall, and Lords Dunsany and Louth. He was initially tutored by his cousin, Patrick Plunkett, who became Catholic bishop of Ardagh and later of Meath.

In 1647, Plunkett travelled to Rome, where he studied in the Irish College, and was ordained a priest in 1654. Students were normally required to return to Ireland, but at the height of Cromwellian persecution Plunkett successfully petitioned to remain, and in 1657 became a professor of theology. In time, anti-Catholicism eased, and in 1669 Plunkett was appointed archbishop of Armagh. He was consecrated discreetly in Ghent, and reached Ireland in 1670.

Plunkett quickly set about reorganising the ravaged Church, though he faced some hostility as an Anglo-Irishman loyal to the crown. He built schools, both for the young and for clergy whom he found 'ignorant in moral theology and controversies'. He tackled drunkenness among the clergy, writing 'Let us remove this defect from an Irish priest, and he will be a saint.' With government approval, he negotiated with the so-called Tories or Rapparees, dispossessed Catholic landowners who had turned to banditry, persuading them into exile as soldiers.

In 1670, he summoned an episcopal conference in Dublin, and he subsequently held numerous synods in his own archdiocese. However, he had a longstanding difference with the archbishop of Dublin, Peter Talbot, over their rival claims to be primate of Ireland. He also antagonised the Franciscans, particularly when he favoured the Dominicans in a property dispute.

With the onset of new persecution in 1673, Plunkett went into hiding for a time, refusing to accept a government edict to register at a seaport and await passage into exile. In 1678, the so-called Popish Plot concocted in England by Titus Oates led to further anti-Catholicism. Talbot was arrested, and Plunkett went into hiding again; the sympathetic viceroy, the Duke of Ormond, had to order Plunkett's arrest after the privy council in London was told he had plotted a French invasion of Ireland.

In December 1679, Plunkett was imprisoned in Dublin Castle, where he gave absolution to the dying Talbot. After the collapse of a trial in Dundalk, Co Louth, he was brought to London; in June 1681, he was found guilty of high treason, largely on the perjured evidence of two disaffected Franciscans. Protesting his innocence, Plunkett was hanged, drawn and quartered at Tyburn on 1 July 1681, the last Catholic martyr in England. He was beatified in 1920 and canonised in 1975, the first new Irish saint for almost seven centuries.

See Plunkett's head is preserved in a shrine at St Peter's Church, West St, Drogheda, Co Louth.
Read Tomás Ó Fiaich & Desmond Forristal, *Oliver Plunkett: his life and letters* (Veritas, Dublin, 1975).

—13—
JONATHAN SWIFT
1667–1745
'THE GREAT DEAN'

Swift was born at 7 Hoey's Court, Dublin, on 30 November 1667. His English father, an official of the King's Inns, had died some months before, and one theory is that Swift was fathered by Sir John Temple, master of the rolls. A wealthy uncle sent him to Kilkenny College, and in 1686 he graduated poorly from Trinity College, Dublin. In 1689, he became private secretary to Sir William Temple (Sir John's son) at Moor Park in Surrey.

He returned to Ireland in 1694, took holy orders, and in 1695 became curate of Kilroot, Co Antrim. In 1696, he returned to Moor Park, where he tutored Esther or Hester Johnson, the beloved 'Stella' of his writings. Ostensibly a housekeeper's daughter, she may have been Temple's child and thus possibly a blood relative of Swift.

Temple died in 1699, and Swift became domestic chaplain to the Earl of Berkeley, lately appointed lord justice in Ireland; he also became vicar of Laracor, near Trim, Co Meath. After Berkeley's recall in 1701, Swift spent much time in England, acquiring a reputation as a wit and pamphleteer. In 1704, he published *A Tale of a Tub*, satirising 'gross corruption in Religion and Learning' and incidentally damaging his chances of ecclesiastical preferment, and *The Battle of the Books*, a defence of classical literature.

Through Temple, Swift had connections with the governing Whigs, and the Church of Ireland authorities commissioned him to seek relief of taxes on their clergy. He was unsuccessful, and in any case distrusted the Whigs for their tolerance of dissenters; however, the Tories granted relief in 1710, and Swift enjoyed a period of considerable political influence, editing the Tory journal, *The Examiner*. Swift's *Journal to Stella* was written during 1710–13, and retailed the gossip and politics of London society; a bequest from Temple had enabled her to move to Ireland, to live in Dublin and at a cottage at Laracor. He also met and infatuated the young Esther or Hester Vanhomrigh, the 'Vanessa' of his long poem *Cadenus and Vanessa* (1713).

Swift had hoped for a bishopric, but in 1713 became dean of St Patrick's Cathedral in Dublin. Initially unpopular, he felt himself exiled 'to die in a rage, like a poisoned rat in a hole', but won popularity as 'The Great Dean' by turning his savage pen to English misrule. In 1720, he advocated a boycott of English manufactures, advising 'Burn everything that comes from England except the coal.' In his anonymous *Drapier's Letters* (1724), he successfully opposed a corrupt Whig scheme to impose a new currency, 'Wood's halfpence'. In 1729, *A Modest Proposal* suggested bitterly that Ireland's wretched and impoverished children might be sold to feed the rich. His major work, however, was *Gulliver's Travels* (1726), a satire directed at the follies of his time which ironically has survived as a children's classic.

Vanessa died of consumption at Celbridge, Co Kildare, in 1723. Stella – 'The truest, most virtuous and most valuable friend' – died in 1727. Swift's last years were unhappy; he suffered from Ménière's Disease, and described himself as 'Deaf, giddy, helpless, left alone'. He was committed to the care of guardians in 1742, and died on 19 October 1745. He left £8,000 to build St Patrick's Hospital as a home for the insane, having written

> He gave what little Wealth he had
> To build a House for Fools and Mad;
> And shew'd by one satyric Touch,
> No Nation wanted it so much.

Swift was the first great Anglo-Irish writer, and an inspiration to Henry Grattan (*qv*) and the 'Protestant nation'. W. B. Yeats (*qv*) was to write: 'Swift haunts me; he is always just round the next corner.'

Visit St Patrick's Cathedral, Patrick St, Dublin (guidebook), where Swift is buried near Stella, and – in a translation of his own Latin epitaph – 'where fierce indignation can no longer rend the heart. Go traveller, and imitate, if you can, this earnest and dedicated champion of liberty.' Nearby is Marsh's Library, used by Swift. Swift's deanery was destroyed by fire in 1781, but was rebuilt, retaining the original cellar and kitchen quarters.
See St Patrick's Hospital, Bow Lane West, Dublin. Busts of Swift in Trinity College and the National Gallery, Dublin. A plaque at the corner of Little and Great Ship Sts, on the wall of Dublin Castle, recalls Swift's now demolished birthplace.
Read Robert Wyse Jackson (ed), *The Best of Swift* (Mercier Press, Cork, 1967) and Denis Donoghue (ed), *Swift Revisited* (Mercier Press, Cork, 1968) are excellent brief introductions to Swift's life and work.

(See plate 1)

—14— TURLOUGH CAROLAN

1670–1738
BLIND HARPER

Carolan (or O'Carolan) was born in 1670 near Nobber, Co Meath. Little is known of his family, who moved to Co Roscommon, where his father worked for the MacDermott Roe family of Alderford, near Ballyfarnon, possibly in their ironworks. Mrs Mary MacDermott Roe provided for Carolan's education, but at eighteen he lost his eyesight from smallpox. His patroness then arranged for him to be taught the harp, and when he was twenty-one provided a horse and servant so that he could travel throughout Ireland.

Music-making was a common occupation of the blind, and Carolan was well received in great houses. He was much more renowned as a composer than for his virtuosity on the harp, and he repaid hospitality by naming tunes after his benefactors – with titles such as 'Planxty Reynolds', 'Planxty Maguire', the planxty being a tune for the harp, and 'Bumper Squire Jones'. He also composed verses in Irish. An early love affair inspired the tune 'Bridget Cruise'; many years later, he recognised the touch of her fingers when climbing into a ferryboat during a pilgrimage to Lough Derg, Co Donegal. In Dublin, he was a friend of Dr Patrick Delany, professor of oratory at Trinity College, and through him of Jonathan Swift (*qv*); Delany translated an Irish verse for which Carolan had written the melody. Italian music was popular in the city, and Carolan was influenced by Corelli, Vivaldi and Geminiani.

Most of the harper's travels were in Ulster and Connacht, and his wife, Mary Maguire, came from Co Fermanagh. They built a small house near Mohill, Co Leitrim, and had seven children. One of his laments was written after her death in 1733. When Carolan himself felt death was near, he made his way to Alderford, where he called for his harp and played his 'Farewell to Music'. On his deathbed, according to one story, he called for a cup of whiskey, but could not drink it; he then kissed the cup, saying that such old friends should not part without a kiss. Carolan died on 25 March 1738. After a wake reputedly attended by ten harpers, he was buried in the MacDermott Roe family chapel at nearby Kilronan Abbey.

More than two hundred of Carolan's melodies have survived. During his lifetime, a volume of his works was published in Dublin, and Delany arranged a further volume after Carolan's death. Edward Bunting (*qv*) later published many of Carolan's melodies. The blind musician was the last of the great Irish harpers, who vanished as the traditional Gaelic culture yielded to the penal laws.

See Kilronan graveyard (2½miles/4 km SE of Ballyfarnon, on the Sligo–Drumshanbo road). Carolan's harp is at Clonalis House, near Castlerea, Co Roscommon (open afternoons, Sat–Mon in May, June, Sept, Wed–Mon in July–Aug). A memorial erected by Sydney Lady Morgan is in St Patrick's Cathedral, Patrick St, Dublin.
Read Donal O'Sullivan, *Carolan: The Life, Times and Music of an Irish Harper* (Routledge & Kegan Paul, two vols, 1958).

—15—

AODHAGÁN Ó RATHAILLE

*c*1670–*c*1726
POOR BARD

Aodhagán Ó Rathaille (or Egan O'Rahilly) was born *c*1670 in the rugged Sliabh Luachra district of Co Kerry. Little is known of his early life, but he was well versed in Latin and English as well as his native tongue, and he may have attended one of the last bardic schools in Killarney. His family were farmers, traditionally under the protection of the MacCarthys, but with new allegiance to Sir Nicholas Brown, 2nd Viscount Kenmare, a Roman Catholic whose Elizabethan forebears had supplanted the Gaelic MacCarthys.

The defeat of the Jacobite cause at Derry, the Boyne and Aughrim in 1689–91 foreshadowed the penal laws of 1695 onwards. Ó Rathaille reached manhood as a civilisation came to an end; in 1691, following the Treaty of Limerick, Gaelic chiefs left Ireland in large numbers to serve as mercenaries in European armies. The poet or bard was left without a patron; unlike the harpist Carolan (*qv*), Ó Rathaille had nothing to offer the Anglo-Irish settlers who replaced the Gaelic lords – though in a poem recalling the past glories of a MacCarthy stronghold, Togher Castle, he was careful to flatter the new occupant.

Gaelic Ireland lingered on more resiliently in the valleys of Munster than in less isolated regions, and Ó Rathaille was one of several Kerry poets whose work is still admired. He was reduced to poverty in later life, recalling in one poem that he had not needed to eat dogfish or periwinkles in his youth. Many poems were elegies in which he listed genealogies going back centuries; some were satires. Most enduring are his lyric poems, particularly 'Gile na Gile' (Brightness of brightness). It is one of his *aisling* or vision poems, and Ireland is represented by a beautiful woman left (in James Clarence Mangan's translation) 'to languish Amid a ruffian horde till the Heroes cross the sea'. The heroes never returned; the Jacobite cause foundered.

Ó Rathaille died *c*1726 without leaving his native Munster. He must have recited at the so-called courts of poetry, occasional gatherings which replaced the bardic schools, and manuscript copies of his poems were widely circulated. In his deathbed poem he prepares 'to follow the beloved among heroes to the grave, Those princes under whom were my ancestors before the death of Christ'.

See Ó Rathaille is buried at Muckross Abbey (2½ miles/4 km S of Killarney) with MacCarthy chiefs. In College St, Killarney, he and three other Kerry poets are commemorated in a monument by Séamus Murphy.

Read Seán Ó Tuama & Thomas Kinsella, *An Duanaire, 1600–1900: Poems of the Dispossessed* (Dolmen Press, Dublin, 1981) is an excellent anthology of Irish poetry, with English translations.

—16— GEORGE BERKELEY

1685–1753 PHILOSOPHER BISHOP

Berkeley was born on 12 March 1685, possibly at Dysart Castle, near Thomastown, Co Kilkenny, where he was brought up, but more probably at Kilcrene, outside Kilkenny town. He was educated at Kilkenny College, before entering Trinity College, Dublin, in 1700. He graduated in 1704, and was elected a fellow in 1707. In 1710, he took holy orders, as was required of fellows.

Trinity College, Dublin, was then more progressive than Oxford or Cambridge universities, and John Locke's *Essay on Human Understanding* (1690) had quickly become part of the philosophy course. Berkeley's study of Locke, and the contradictions he detected, led him to become an 'immaterialist', denying the existence of matter and arguing that things depended for their existence on being perceived: *esse est percipi*. His major contributions to philosophy, establishing a European reputation, were published in a brief period: *An Essay towards a New Theory of Vision* (1709), *A Treatise concerning the Principles of Human Knowledge* (1710), his masterpiece, and *Three Dialogues between Hylas and Philonous* (1713).

Granted leave in 1713, he quickly made a mark in London's drawing-rooms and coffee-houses, enjoying the friendship of Swift (*qv*), Pope, Addison and Steele. He also travelled widely in France and Italy. Berkeley returned to Trinity College, Dublin, in 1721, but his hopes rested in the Church. In 1724, he was appointed Dean of Derry and immediately launched an ambitious project for a college in Bermuda. 'Westward the Course of Empire takes its Way' he wrote in a poem; he hoped to prepare colonists' sons for the ministry and to educate young American Indians.

Promised a government grant of £20,000, Berkeley sailed for the New World in 1728, having lately married Anne Forster, daughter of an Irish chief justice. He first settled in Newport, Rhode Island, but returned to England in 1731 when it became apparent that the grant would never materialise. Meanwhile, he had popularised his philosophical ideas in America, made gifts to Yale and Harvard universities, and written *Alciphron* (1732) to defend Anglican Christianity against free thinkers.

In 1734, Berkeley became Bishop of Cloyne, Co Cork. The most influential publication of his later years was *The Querist* (three volumes, 1735–7), which posed almost six hundred questions about social and economic conditions in Ireland. He also became an advocate of 'tar-water', a resinous medicine which he described in *Siris* (1744) as 'so mild and benign and proportioned to the human condition, as to warm without heating, to cheer but not inebriate'. Ill health caused his resignation in 1752. He moved to Oxford, dying there on 14 January 1753. The most famous tribute had already been paid in a poem by Alexander Pope: 'To Berkeley, every Virtue under Heav'n'.

See The thirteenth-century cathedral at Cloyne contains a memorial to Berkeley.
Read A. A. Luce, *The Life of George Berkeley, Bishop of Cloyne* (Nelson, 1949); J. O. Urmson, *Berkeley* (Oxford University Press, 1982).

—17—

PEG WOFFINGTON

*c*1718–1760
A STAR IS BORN

Margaret Woffington was born in Dublin, possibly on 18 October 1718 but perhaps as early as 1714. Her bricklayer father died within a few years, and her mother raised her two daughters precariously, finally selling watercress in the streets. Peg also sold cress; a pretty child, she attracted the attention of Madame Violante, who recruited her into her company of juveniles, performing in a booth in George's Lane. At twelve, she played Polly Peachum in *The Beggar's Opera*. In 1732, she accompanied Violante to London, playing Macheath at the Haymarket, but returned to Dublin after the venture failed.

Peg was next apprenticed to the famous Smock Alley theatre, under Francis Elrington; when he opened a new Theatre Royal in Aungier Street, she played Rose in Farquhar's *The Recruiting Officer*. An actress's illness allowed her to play Ophelia in *Hamlet*, and she soon became a leading performer. When eventually she played Sylvia in *The Recruiting Officer*, her success in soldier's uniform set a pattern for many future performances. Her greatest role in breeches, which displayed her fine figure, was Sir Harry Wildair in Farquhar's *The Constant Couple*. 'I have played the part so often that half the town believes me to be a real man,' she once confided to an actor, James Quin, who replied, 'Madame, the other half knows you to be a woman'.

In 1740, Peg took London by storm, repeating at Covent Garden her roles in Farquhar's comedies. The following year, Mrs Woffington (as she was now billed) appeared at Drury Lane, playing among other parts Cordelia to the King Lear of a new young actor, David Garrick. After a summer season at Smock Alley in 1742, they returned to London as lovers and set up home in Bow Street. Garrick was as parsimonious as Peg was openhanded, however, and after contemplating marriage they parted in 1744. Their professional relationship also soured, and in 1748 Peg moved to Covent Garden, where her abrasiveness made enemies of such actresses as Kitty Clive and George Anne Bellamy. Meanwhile, she had seen her sister Polly, educated in France at Peg's expense, married to an earl's son.

In 1751, Peg returned triumphantly to Smock Alley, now managed by Thomas Sheridan, godson of Jonathan Swift and father of Richard Brinsley Sheridan (*qqv*); when he founded the Beefsteak Club, where influential patrons dined with theatrical and literary figures, Peg became president. She returned to London in 1754, enjoying new success at Covent Garden, though her feud with Mrs Bellamy once caused Peg to drive her rival off the stage. In 1757, her health was declining, and she collapsed on stage while playing Rosalind in *As You Like It*. It was her last performance; she died on 28 March 1760. She was buried at Teddington, where she had lived and had endowed alms-houses.

Read Janet Dunbar, *Peg Woffington and her World* (Heinemann, 1968).

(See plate 2)

—18—
ARTHUR GUINNESS
1725–1803
STOUT FELLOW

Guinness was born at Celbridge, Co Kildare, in 1725. His father was land steward to the Archbishop of Cashel, Dr Arthur Price, and brewed beer for workers on the estate. When Price died in 1752, he left £100 each to the two Guinnesses, which may have encouraged the young man to lease a brewery in Leixlip, Co Kildare, in 1756. Three years later, he left this brewery in charge of his younger brother, Richard, and took over another one at St James's Gate in Dublin.

He began by brewing beer or ale, and within eight years was master of the Dublin Corporation of Brewers; he also owned flour mills at nearby Kilmainham. In 1761, he married Olivia Whitmore, who was related to Henry Grattan (*qv*), and ten of their twenty-one children lived to establish a dynasty which has spread into many activities and countries. The family's long association with St Patrick's Cathedral began with a gift of 250 guineas for the chapel schools, and the city of Dublin enjoyed other benefactions. Guinness also became governor of the Meath Hospital, and worked to improve prison conditions.

There was, however, one dispute with Dublin Corporation, whose investigators concluded that Guinness was drawing more free water than his lease permitted; in 1775, the brewer seized a pickaxe to defend his supplies from the sheriff, and eventually reached a peaceful settlement after protracted litigation. Duties on beer proved another problem, and in 1795 Guinness was able to enlist Grattan's oratory in persuading the government to remove the burden.

In 1778, Guinness began to brew porter – the darker beer containing roasted barley and first drunk by London porters – and exploited Ireland's new canals to extend his market. In 1799, he brewed ale for the last time; it proved a wise choice, for the brewery's sales of porter increased threefold during the Napoleonic

Wars. In time, St James's Gate would become the largest porter and stout brewery in the world, its 'extra stout porter' becoming known simply as stout.

Guinness's eldest son, Hosea, had become rector of nearby St Werburgh's Church. However, three other sons became successful brewers, and he gradually handed over control to them. In 1764, he had bought a country home, Beaumont, at Drumcondra, now a suburb of Dublin, and he spent his last years there. He died on 23 January 1803.

Visit Guinness visitors' centre and museum, Thomas St, Dublin (open Mon–Fri).
See Guinness's town house, 1 Thomas St, is now part of the entrance to the brewery. Beaumont is a convalescent home.
Read Peter Walsh, *Guinness* (Eason, Dublin, 1980), a brief introduction to the Guinnesses and their brewery; Frederic Mullally, *The Silver Salver: The Story of the Guinness Family* (Granada, 1981).

(See plate 3)

—19—
OLIVER GOLDSMITH
1728–1774
THE CITIZEN OF THE WORLD

Accounts of Goldsmith's birth vary, but the entry in a family Bible places it in Pallas, Co Longford, on 10 November 1728. His father, Rev Charles Goldsmith, became rector of nearby Kilkenny West in 1730, and Goldsmith spent his childhood at Lissoy parsonage in Co Westmeath. His years in the Irish Midlands were to inspire his most famous poem, *The Deserted Village.* Goldsmith was much influenced by the local schoolmaster, Thomas Byrne ('And still they gazed and still the wonder grew, That one small head could carry all he knew'), an ex-soldier who encouraged his early interest in poetry.

In 1745, he entered Trinity College, Dublin, as a sizar or poor scholar, but his academic career was distinguished for scrapes more than study. On graduating, he spent three aimless years before going to Edinburgh to study medicine. Unsuccessful there, he continued his studies in Leyden, Holland, then embarked on a walking tour in Europe before arriving penniless in London in 1756.

There he found work as physician, schoolmaster and chemist's assistant before beginning to write for the *Monthly Review* and other periodicals. His output was prolific and much was hack work, but as the lexicographer Samuel Johnson wrote in the epitaph on Goldsmith's memorial in Westminster Abbey, 'Nullum quod tetigit non ornavit' (He touched nothing which he did not adorn). The first real success was his amusingly reflective 'Chinese Letters' in the *Public Ledger*, collected in 1762 as *The Citizen of the World*. In 1763, he was invited to become a founder member of Johnson's famous 'Club' for artists and writers, which met in the Turk's Head tavern in Soho; other members included Edmund Burke (*qv*) and the painter, Sir Joshua Reynolds, his closest friend.

Goldsmith's poem, *The Traveller*, was well received in 1764, and in 1766 came his first novel, *The Vicar of Wakefield*, which was translated into many languages. A play, *The Good-natur'd Man*, had only modest success in 1768, but in 1770 *The Deserted Village* went quickly into five editions with its sombre portrait of 'Sweet Auburn! Loveliest village of the plain' drawn from memories of Lissoy. His last triumph was the farce, *She Stoops to Conquer*, staged in 1773. Goldsmith was both generous and a gambler, and financial worries probably aggravated the fever from which he died (owing £2,000) on 4 April 1774. Asked at the end by his doctor if his mind was at ease, he replied 'No, it is not.'

Visit Ruins of Lissoy parsonage, 'The village preacher's modest mansion', 5 miles/8 km SW of Ballymahon, Co Longford; nearby sites of school, 'busy mill', alehouse and 'decent church'. Also Pallas, 2 miles/3 km NW of Ballymahon. In nearby Ardagh, a plaque marks 'the best house in the village', in which young Goldsmith sought lodgings thinking it an inn; the incident provided the plot of *She Stoops to Conquer*.
See Statue by John Henry Foley in front of Trinity College, Dublin.
Read A. Lytton Sells, *Oliver Goldsmith: His Life and Works* (Allen & Unwin, 1974); John Ginger, *The Notable Man: The Life and*

Times of Oliver Goldsmith (Hamish Hamilton, 1977). The Goldsmith Press edition of *The Deserted Village* (The Curragh, Ireland, 1978) includes a useful chronology and introduction by Desmond Egan.

(See plate 4)

—20— EDMUND BURKE

1729–1797 POLITICAL PHILOSOPHER

Burke was born at 12 Arran Quay, Dublin, probably on 1 January 1729. His father was a prosperous Protestant attorney; his mother was a Roman Catholic from Ballyduff, Co Cork. After graduating from Trinity College, Dublin, in 1748 Burke studied law at the Middle Temple in London. However, his interests were literary, and in 1756 a publisher accepted *A Vindication of Natural Society*, a satirical work which foreshadowed his later onslaughts on the destructive rationalism which begot the French Revolution.

In 1757, he married Jane Nugent of Bath, an Irish doctor's daughter; a Catholic, she thereafter adhered to the Anglican Church. Soon afterwards, Burke published *The Sublime and the Beautiful*, a study of aesthetics. In 1759, he became first editor of the *Annual Register*, an immediately influential world review.

Burke also became private secretary to W. G. Hamilton MP, chief secretary in Ireland during 1761–4. When they quarrelled in 1765, the Irish adventurer became private secretary to the new Whig prime minister, Lord Rockingham. He entered Westminster in 1766 as MP for the rotten borough of Wendover, and held this and other seats until 1794; he proved a forceful if indiscreet orator, though in later years his diffuseness earned him the nickname 'Dinner Bell'. More than any contemporary, Burke raised the level of political debate by invoking standards of justice and by arguing from moral principle rather than expediency, yet his approach to political issues was essentially pragmatic. He articulated best the role of MP as representative rather than delegate, fostered the party system, and did much to abolish corrupting sinecures.

He was ill served by the financial jobbery of his relatives, however, and his own shady manoeuvrings tarnished his reputation. Burke's finances were often precarious – not least because he bought an estate near Beaconsfield, in Buckinghamshire, for £20,000 in 1768 – and his lack of practical judgement, as much as his unaristocratic background, probably denied him high office. 'Though equal to all things, for all things unfit,' wrote his friend Goldsmith (*qv*).

Every major political problem engaged Burke's attention. He championed individual liberty against George III's attempts to restore the influence of the monarchy. He urged a conciliatory policy towards the American colonists before the War of Independence. He fought for better government in British India, and in 1786 moved the impeachment of the former governor-general, Warren Hastings. In the prescient book which brought him a European reputation, *Reflections on the Revolution in France* (1790), Burke saw the threat posed to the ordered liberty of England; however, his conservative ideas split the Whigs, ended a long friendship with Charles James Fox, and evoked a famous reply in Thomas Paine's *Rights of Man*.

On retiring from the Commons in 1794, Burke turned to Ireland, whose economic and parliamentary independence he had always supported. His son Richard succeeded him as MP for Malton, and was to become chief secretary in Ireland; the new lord lieutenant was Lord Fitzwilliam, nephew of Rockingham and much under Edmund's influence. Richard had preceded Wolfe Tone (*qv*) as agent of the Catholic Committee, and his father looked forward to promoting Catholic emancipation. However, Richard died suddenly of consumption, and the tactless Fitzwilliam was quickly recalled from Dublin in 1795; further reform was halted, and as in America the stage was set for revolution. A disappointed Burke died at Beaconsfield on 9 July 1797.

See Statue by John Henry Foley in front of Trinity College, Dublin.
Read Sir Philip Magnus, *Edmund Burke: A Life* (Murray, 1939); C. B. Macpherson, *Burke* (Oxford University Press, 1980).

(See plate 5)

1 Bust of Jonathan Swift by Patrick Cunningham, in St Patrick's Cathedral, Dublin

2 Peg Woffington, painted by John Lewis

3 Arthur Guinness (artist unknown)

4 Statue of Oliver Goldsmith by John Henry Foley, in Trinity College, Dublin

5 Statue of Edmund Burke, also (see plate 4) by John Henry Foley and also in Trinity College, Dublin

6 The Four Courts, Dublin, designed by James Gandon

7 The restored birthplace of Edmund Ignatius Rice, near Callan, Co Kilkenny

8 Theobald Wolfe Tone (artist unknown)

—21—

FREDERICK HERVEY

4th EARL OF BRISTOL

1730–1803

THE EARL BISHOP

Hervey was born at Ickworth, the family seat in Suffolk, on 1 August 1730. Educated at Westminster School and Corpus Christi College, Cambridge, he interrupted his studies in 1752 to marry Elizabeth Danvers, a baronet's daughter. In 1755, he took holy orders, and by 1763 he was a royal chaplain. In 1766, his brother George, the 2nd Earl, was appointed lord lieutenant of Ireland; Frederick became his chaplain, and was then appointed to the minor bishopric of Cloyne, Co Cork, in 1767. When the more profitable bishopric of Derry fell vacant in 1768, George persuaded his successor to translate Frederick. The latter reputedly heard the news while playing leapfrog, and declared 'Gentlemen, I have surpassed you all. I have jumped from Cloyne to Derry.'

Two of Hervey's three great houses were built in his new diocese: Downhill, overlooking Lough Foyle; and the unfinished Ballyscullion, at nearby Lough Beg. The third was a reconstruction of Ickworth, which his wife (who left him in 1782) considered 'a stupendous monument to folly'. He filled his houses with Italian and Flemish art treasures; another interest was geology, stimulated when one of his arms was injured during an eruption of Vesuvius. Hervey also introduced church reforms, promoting clergy within his diocese and establishing pension funds; he added spires to make churches more visible, and pressed for the easing of penal laws against Roman Catholics. He succeeded to the earldom in 1779.

The threat of a French invasion led to the formation of companies of Volunteers, an armed militia which strengthened the political and economic demands of the emerging 'Protestant nation'. In 1783, the Earl Bishop became colonel of the Derry Volunteers, and received an ovation in several towns before arriving in Dublin for a Volunteer convention. However, a deception by Sir Boyle Roche (*qv*) thwarted his hopes of committing the Volunteers to Catholic emancipation.

In 1785, he left Ireland again; he suffered badly from gout, and thereafter was seldom in his diocese. His eccentricities increased, and he associated with such courtesans as Lady Hamilton and Countess Lichtenau. Once when a woman of easy virtue entered Lady Hamilton's salon, he retired saying it was permissible for a bishop to visit a sinner but not to be seen in a brothel. Many European hotels were named after him. He died near Rome on 8 July 1803.

Visit Mussenden Temple, near the ruins of Downhill (1 mile/1.5 km W of Castlerock, Co Londonderry), is a National Trust property (guidebook; open afternoons, April–Sept, Sat–Thurs). A library and summerhouse, named after a female cousin, it is derived from the Temples of Vesta at Tivoli.
See The portico from Ballyscullion is incorporated in St George's Church, High St, Belfast.

—22—
JAMES GANDON
1743–1823
ARCHITECT OF DUBLIN

Gandon was born in London on 29 February 1743. His father, of French Huguenot stock, improvidently squandered his time and fortune on experiments in alchemy and in studying Rosicrucianism. Gandon showed artistic talent at school, and entered a drawing academy in St Martin's Lane, where in 1757 he won a Society of Arts award. He was apprenticed to the architect Sir William Chambers, then set up on his own account in 1765. Four years later, he won the first gold medal in architecture awarded by the Royal Academy.

Chambers designed a number of Irish houses, including Charlemont House, the eventual Dublin home of the paintings collected by Sir Hugh Lane (*qv*). Through his office, Gandon made influential acquaintances in Ireland, and in 1768 he was runner-up in the competition to design the Royal Exchange (now the City Hall) in Dublin. Lord Carlow encouraged him to submit plans for a new Custom House, and in 1781 he was invited by John Beresford, the chief commissioner of revenue, to superintend the building work.

Gandon gave up his profitable English practice to settle in Dublin, where he found only two architects of repute; one was Thomas Cooley, whose Royal Exchange had just been completed. Within a few years, Gandon matched the political and commercial vitality of the period by producing some of the finest eighteenth-century architecture. The Custom House itself proved a difficult project, not merely for its waterlogged site but because of hostile mobs and drunken workers demanding higher wages; Gandon carried a sword whenever he inspected the work.

The building was completed in 1791, notable features being the statue of Commerce and sixteen heads of river gods sculpted by Edward Smyth, who embellished many of Gandon's later buildings. By then, Gandon had designed Waterford's courthouse and jail, extensions to the parliament building in College Green, Carlisle (now O'Connell) Bridge, the Royal Military Infirmary in Phoenix Park and supremely the new Four Courts. This second masterpiece, on Dublin's quays, was completed in 1802.

Gandon's third great building, the King's Inns in Henrietta Street, was begun in 1795. He returned to London in 1797, rightly fearing the rising which occurred the following year, but was back in Dublin in 1799. He retired in 1808, leaving an associate to complete the King's Inns. Gandon's last years were spent at his house, Canonbrook, Lucan, Co Dublin. He continued to prepare plans for private houses, triumphal arches and improvements in Dublin architecture, but nothing was built. He died on 24 December 1823, and was buried in Drumcondra churchyard, Dublin, with his old friend, the antiquarian Francis Grose.

(See plate 6)

—23—

SIR BOYLE ROCHE

1743–1807
THE IRISH 'BULL'

Roche, member of an old Anglo-Norman family, was born in 1743. Having served with distinction in the army, he became MP for Tralee in 1776. He held this and other seats until the Acts of Union in 1800, and his consistent support of the government gained him a baronetcy in 1782. He was also chamberlain to the vice-regal court.

During the 1783 convention of Volunteers in Dublin, Frederick Hervey, Earl of Bristol (*qv*), argued for extending the franchise to Roman Catholics. An opponent of emancipation, George Ogle, produced a letter denying that Catholics sought further concessions, and Roche confirmed that he himself had received it from a leading Catholic, Lord Kenmare. The convention consequently took no action, to the relief of Dublin Castle, even though it later emerged that Roche had lied. Unperturbed, Roche explained that he had 'resolved on a bold stroke . . . authorised only by a knowledge of the sentiments of the persons in question'. It was his most notable political act, but he is better remembered as the perpetrator of Irish 'bulls'.

It was not unusual for members of the government to write Roche's speeches, which he then committed to memory. While he usually retained the substance of a speech, he inclined towards verbal contradictions which have found a secure place in dictionaries of quotations. Best recalled, perhaps, is 'Mr Speaker, I smell a rat; I see him forming in the air and darkening the sky; but I'll nip him in the bud.' He once asked the speaker 'How could I be in two places at once unless I were a bird?' and insisted that 'Half the lies our opponents tell about us are untrue.' Attributed to him are 'What has posterity done for us?' and 'All along the untrodden paths of the future I can see the footprints of an unseen hand.'

Roche was an active supporter of the Union, declaring that his love for England and Ireland was such that he would have the two sister nations embracing like one brother. However, he spoke prophetically when he warned that 'The cup of Ireland's miseries has been overflowing for centuries, and is not yet full.' Roche died at his home at 63 Eccles Street, Dublin, on 5 June 1807.

—24—
HENRY GRATTAN
1746–1820
INDEPENDENT PARLIAMENTARIAN

Grattan was born on 4 July 1746. His father was recorder of Dublin for many years; his mother was daughter of a chief justice. On graduating from Trinity College, Dublin, in 1767 Grattan was admitted to the Middle Temple in London to study law. He spent much of his time at Westminster, admiring the oratory of Edmund Burke (*qv*), and his landlady complained of him walking in the garden at night addressing an invisible 'Mr Speaker'.

Returning to Dublin in 1772, he was called to the Irish Bar. In 1775, the influential Earl of Charlemont offered him a vacant seat for the borough of Charlemont, Co Armagh. Grattan entered the Irish parliament just as Henry Flood, for some years leader of the 'patriot party', had accepted government office in the mistaken belief that he could better influence policy. He quickly took Flood's place, and in 1779 persuaded the British Government to remove most of the restrictions on Irish trade; in this, he was supported by the rise of a Protestant militia, the Volunteers. In 1782, Westminster conceded Grattan's demand for Irish parliamentary independence.

A grateful Irish parliament voted Grattan £50,000, which he unwisely accepted, and, on marrying Henrietta Fitzgerald, he settled at Tinnehinch, Co Wicklow. Flood, now out of office, undermined Grattan's leadership by calling for further assurances of Irish independence, and Westminster conceded the 1783 Act of Renunciation. It proved a worthless gain, however, and impaired the unity of the 'Protestant nation'; the two rivals had to be restrained from fighting a duel.

'Grattan's Parliament' coincided with commercial prosperity and the flowering of Georgian Dublin. It eased penal restrictions on the Catholic majority, and some were allowed to vote but not to sit in parliament. Although refusing office, Grattan became a privy counsellor in 1790. He believed that 'the Irish Protestant should never be free until the Irish Catholic ceased to be a slave', but in 1795 the recall of the reforming lord lieutenant, Lord Fitzwilliam, ended the prospect of further reform. In poor health and opposed to both the government and the revolutionary United Irishmen, Grattan retired from parliament in 1797. He returned in 1800 as MP for the borough of Wicklow to speak in Volunteer uniform against the proposed Union with Great Britain. Later, he fought and wounded the chancellor of the exchequer, Isaac Corry, who had accused him of abetting rebellion.

In 1805, at the instigation of Fitzwilliam and Charles James Fox, Grattan entered the Westminster parliament, representing first the English borough of Malton and from 1806 Dublin. He devoted the rest of his political life unavailingly to Catholic emancipation, and died in London on 4 June 1820. He was buried in Westminster Abbey.

See Statue by John Henry Foley at College Green, Dublin, close to the old parliament building (now the Bank of Ireland). A plaque marks his Dublin home at 56 St Stephen's Green.
Read Stephen Gwynn, *Henry Grattan and His Times* (Browne & Nolan, Dublin, 1939).

—25—
BRIAN MERRIMAN
*c*1747–1805
A SINGULAR POET

Merriman (in some Irish manuscripts, Brian Mac Giolla Meidhre) was born *c*1747, probably near Ennistymon, Co Clare. Little is known of his early life, but his father may have been a small farmer. He would have been educated at a hedge school or perhaps by a priest, and he was an accomplished fiddler. By 1770, he had become a teacher at Feakle, Co Clare, then a poor and isolated area inaccessible to coaches. He also farmed twenty acres, and won prizes from the Dublin Society for growing flax. He was close to forty when he married.

Merriman's fame rests on a single poem in Irish of 1,206 lines, *Cúirt an Mheán Oíche* or *The Midnight Court*, written *c*1780. It was widely circulated in manuscript during his life, and published in Dublin towards the end of the century as *Mediae Noctis Consilium*. The poem has attracted many translators, among them Percy Arland Ussher, Frank O'Connor (*qv*), the 6th Earl of Longford and Thomas Kinsella; Cumann Merriman, the Merriman Society, holds a summer school each August in Co Clare. Apart from two lyrics attributed to him, *The Midnight Court* is all that has survived of Merriman's work. No one knows if he wrote anything else; certainly, he lived far from the courts of poetry which survived in Co Kerry and which might have encouraged him.

In the poem, the author is walking by Lough Graney when he is summoned to stand trial at a fairy court in nearby Feakle, where he is accused of remaining a bachelor. The lyrical opening quickly gives way to the bawdy comedy of the trial, covering such subjects as promiscuity, illegitimacy, impotence and the celibacy of clergy. After the evidence of a disconsolate spinster and a deceived old man, the poet is stripped for punishment by the assembled women – and then wakes up. Merriman's humour often recalls his Scottish contemporary, Robert Burns; long after his death, he was to trouble the Irish Censorship Board more than any other writer.

Late in life, Merriman moved to the city of Limerick, where he died on 27 July 1805. One of the few certainties about his life is the entry in the *General Advertiser and Limerick Gazette*: 'Died on Saturday morning, in Old Clare-street, after a few hours' illness, Mr Bryan Merryman, teacher of Mathematics, etc.' He was buried in Feakle.

See A plaque marks the old graveyard in Feakle where Merriman is buried; his grave has not been identified.
Read Brendan Kennelly (ed), *The Penguin Book of Irish Verse* (1970) contains O'Connor's version of *The Midnight Court*.

—26—
JOHN PHILPOT CURRAN
1750–1817
THE GREAT ADVOCATE

Curran was born on 24 July 1750 in Newmarket, Co Cork, where his father was steward to the wealthy Aldworth family. In boyhood, as later, he was small, ugly and in delicate health, but his intellect attracted the local rector, who helped to pay for an education in Midleton College. Winning a sizarship to Trinity College, Dublin, in 1769, Curran intended to enter the Church, but he was deflected by the dissipations of student life and opted instead for the Bar.

In 1773, he entered the Middle Temple in London, where he practised oratory at debating clubs; although handicapped by a shrill voice and a stutter, he had a gift of invective when angered. In 1774, he married the daughter of a Newmarket doctor, and her small dowry helped them withstand early poverty when he was admitted to the Irish Bar in 1775. When she ran off with a clergyman in 1793, a subsequent court case exposed Curran's own infidelities.

Curran's career flourished on the notorious Munster Circuit, where corruption prevailed and perverse verdicts were common; a fellow advocate, Barry Yelverton, was once waylaid by his acquitted client, who stole back his fee. In 1780, he represented a Catholic priest against the influential Lord Doneraile, who had horsewhipped him; Curran's fame was assured when his eloquence moved a Protestant jury to award the priest damages of thirty guineas. In 1782, he was appointed a King's Counsel.

In 1779, Curran had become prior of 'The Monks of the Screw', a political dining club he and Yelverton founded in Dublin; Henry Grattan (*qv*) was a member. In 1783, he was elected MP for Kilbeggan, Co Westmeath, a pocket borough owned by an old friend, Richard Longfield; however, his views were more radical than his patron's, and in 1785 he bought a seat at Rathcormack, Co Cork, which he held until 1797. Among his causes were penal reform, alleviation of peasant poverty, and Catholic emancipation.

In 1785, he fought a duel with the attorney-general, John Fitzgibbon, and his chancery practice declined after the latter became lord chancellor in 1789. However, Curran prospered in other courts, and was seldom bettered for wit or insult. A rival advocate, 'Bully' Egan, threatened to put the diminutive Curran in his pocket. 'If you do that,' came the reply, 'you'll have more law in your pocket than you ever had in your head.' A judge afflicted with ague brought the remark 'You may have observed his lordship shaking his head while I have been speaking, but I can assure you, gentlemen of the jury, that there is nothing in it.' Curran's most famous saying was entirely serious, when in a legal case over the election of Dublin's lord mayor he warned 'The condition upon which God hath given liberty to man is eternal vigilance; which condition if he break, servitude is at once the consequence of his crime and the punishment of his guilt.'

Curran defended a number of United Irishmen before and after the 1798 rising, with varying success and at some personal risk. However, following the fiasco of the 1803 rising, he coldly refused to represent Robert Emmet (*qv*), who had courted his daughter Sarah; his house at Rathfarnham, Co Dublin, was searched for evidence of treason, and Curran had to protest his own innocence. In 1806, Curran was appointed master of the Irish rolls. He retired in 1814, and died at Brompton, Middlesex, on 14 October 1817, earning an epitaph from Daniel O'Connell (*qv*) that 'There was never so honest an Irishman.' Curran was buried in London, but in 1834 his body was reinterred in Glasnevin cemetery in Dublin.

See Bust in St Patrick's Cathedral, Dublin; sarcophagus at Glasnevin.

Read Leslie Hale, *John Philpot Curran: His Life and Times* (Cape, 1958).

—27—

RICHARD BRINSLEY SHERIDAN

1751–1816
DRAMATIST UNRIVALLED

Sheridan was born at 12 Dorset Street Upper, Dublin, on 30 October 1751. His father, Thomas Sheridan, was an actor who became manager of the Theatre Royal in Dublin's Smock Alley; his mother, Frances Sheridan, wrote novels and plays. Sheridan's early years were spent in the city, but his schooling had scarcely begun when in 1759 he joined his parents in England, where his father was developing a new career as educationist and lecturer on elocution. He never returned to Ireland.

After some unhappy years at Harrow school, Sheridan moved in 1770 with his family to Bath, where his poems began to appear in local journals. In 1772, he eloped to France with Eliza Linley, an attractive young singer. They married near Calais, but the ceremony was invalid and Eliza seems to have been more concerned to escape an unwelcome suitor, with whom Sheridan later fought two duels, suffering severe wounds in the second. Thomas Sheridan tried to separate the young couple, but they were legally married on 13 April 1773.

Eliza's voice could have provided a comfortable income, but Sheridan determined to make quick money from the theatre. The outcome was *The Rivals*, performed at Covent Garden on 17 January 1775. The first night was far from a triumph, but after some rewriting and a change in the cast the play was well received and characters such as Mrs Malaprop and Sir Lucius O'Trigger began to entertain generations of theatregoers. In a few prolific years, Sheridan wrote *St Patrick's Day* (1775); *The Duenna* (1775), a comic opera with music by Eliza's father, Thomas Linley; *A Trip to Scarborough* (1777), adapted from Vanbrugh's *The Relapse*; *The School for Scandal* (1777), his comic masterpiece; *The Camp* (1778); and *The Critic* (1779).

In 1776, Sheridan had taken over management of the Theatre Royal in Drury Lane from David Garrick, and all his later plays were performed there. However, despite his new reputation as the finest playwright since Shakespeare, he had developed a stronger interest in public affairs. In 1780, he was elected MP for Stafford, and subsequently held minor offices in Whig governments; Edmund Burke (*qv*) and Charles James Fox were intimate friends. In politics, Sheridan was sympathetic to the American and French revolutions and to the freedom of the press, and he energetically opposed the Union of Great Britain and Ireland; his most famous speech, lasting almost six hours in 1787, urged the impeachment of Warren Hastings.

Although he contributed to the production of new plays, Sheridan's only other play was *Pizarro* (1799), an adaptation of a German tragedy with which he sought to restore Drury Lane's ailing fortunes. The theatre was eventually destroyed by fire in 1809, adding to Sheridan's financial difficulties, and he lost his seat in Parliament in 1812. Eliza had died in 1792, and in 1795 he married Esther Ogle, twenty-three years younger and a less sympathetic partner. His last years were uncomfortable; he drank too much, fell out with old friends, and was beset by debts when he died on 7 July 1816. None the less, he was given a grand funeral and buried in Poets' Corner at Westminster Abbey. The poet, Lord Byron, advised Thomas Moore (*qv*), an early biographer: 'Recollect that he was an Irishman and a clever fellow, and that we have had some very pleasant days with him.'

See A plaque marks Sheridan's birthplace.
Read Madeleine Bingham, *Sheridan: The Track of a Comet* (Allen & Unwin, 1972).

—28— RICHARD MARTIN

1754–1834
'HUMANITY DICK'

Martin was born in February 1754. His family was one of the powerful 'tribes of Galway', and his father had lately turned Protestant to secure his lands. Martin was raised at Dangan, on the outskirts of Galway, and educated at Harrow and Trinity College, Cambridge. He was MP for Jamestown, Co Leitrim, from 1776 to 1783. Called to the Irish Bar in 1781, Martin appeared in only one case, representing Charles Fitzgerald against his brother George 'Fighting' Fitzgerald, who had shot a wolfhound, and with whom Martin later fought several duels. He then became a magistrate, commanded the Galway Volunteers and a troop of yeomanry, and was commonly called 'King of Connemara'.

His first wife was Elizabeth Vesey, his stepmother's niece, whom he married in 1777. She later infatuated Wolfe Tone (*qv*) when he tutored Martin's stepbrothers and joined in the family's amateur theatricals, then left her husband for another man. Beset with debts, Martin took refuge in Ballynahinch Castle, an inaccessible house (now a hotel) in Connemara. When his father died in 1794, he inherited an estate covering one-third of Co Galway. In 1796, he married Harriet Evans, author of *Historic Tales* and later of a novel, *Helen of Glenross*. He returned to Parliament in 1798 as MP for Lanesborough, Co Leitrim, and supported the Act of Union in 1800. In 1801, he entered Westminster as MP for Co Galway, holding the seat, with only one break, until 1826.

Martin had hoped the Union would bring Catholic emancipation, but it was not achieved until 1829. He was also disappointed in his efforts to remove the death penalty for forgery, and to permit prisoners accused of capital crimes to be represented by counsel. However, he had a memorable success in 1822, when parliament passed his Ill-Treatment of Cattle Bill, the first British measure for the protection of animals. In 1824, he was a founder of the (now Royal) Society for the Prevention of Cruelty to Animals, and was famous for his readiness to defend any passing animal against a cruel master.

It was the Prince Regent (later King George IV) who nicknamed him 'Humanity'. There was a temporary breach in their friendship over Martin's sympathy towards George's estranged consort, Queen Caroline, but the King later greeted Martin warmly in Dublin when he found he had survived a shipwreck. Martin was unseated by petition after an election victory in 1826, and escaped his creditors by settling in Boulogne, in France, where he died on 6 January 1834. A year later, his Act was extended to cover cruelty to all domestic animals.

Read Shevawn Lynam, *Humanity Dick: A Biography of Richard Martin, M.P., 1754–1834* (Hamish Hamilton, 1975).

—29—

SIR JONAH BARRINGTON

1760–1834
RISE AND FALL

Barrington was born at Knapton, near Abbeyleix, Co Laois, in 1760. He was the fourth of sixteen children, and his family lived in a spendthrift atmosphere not unlike the Castle Rackrent described by Maria Edgeworth (*qv*). He was originally destined for the army, but declined the offer of an ensign's commission when he learned that his prospective regiment was about to see service in America. Instead, on graduating from Trinity College, Dublin, he was called to the Bar. More noted for his social graces than for his knowledge of law, he took silk in 1793 and became an admiralty court judge in 1798.

Meanwhile, he had become MP for Tuam, Co Galway, in the Irish parliament in 1790, and later recalled that 'I felt myself an entirely independent representative of an equally independent nation – as a man assuming his proper station in life, not acquiring a new one.' He lost his seat in 1797, but was returned for Clogher, Co Tyrone, in 1798. Barrington generally aligned himself with the government; looking at the Whig opposition, he felt that 'amidst such an assemblage of talent I had but little right to expect eminence, and still less probability of acquiring professional advancement, even if my friends should become victorious'.

He did oppose the Union, however, although offered the post of solicitor-general if he voted for it. Inconsistently, he acted as government agent in offering other MPs inducements to support the measure. He was knighted in 1807. Between 1805 and 1810, when his extravagance plunged him into debt, Barrington misappropriated sums of money which had been paid into his court, but it was not until 1830 that a commission of inquiry confirmed his theft. He was immediately stripped of office, and left the country. He died at Versailles, in France, on 8 April 1834.

In later life, Barrington augmented his income by publishing his reminiscences, notably *Personal Sketches of his own Time* (three volumes, 1827–32) and *The Rise and Fall of the Irish Nation* (1833). The sketches are the most enduring, and give a racy and amusing picture of that Anglo-Irish society in which he distinguished 'half-mounted' gentlemen, gentlemen 'every inch of them' and gentlemen 'to the backbone', each class earning different degrees of respect from the common people. It was a world of idlers educated to little other than riding, cards and claret, and where 'Pistols and cudgels and horsewhips were in every young man's hands at the time.' Barrington was a not untypical product of this world.

See A plaque marks Barrington's home at 14 Harcourt St, Dublin.

—30—

EDMUND IGNATIUS RICE

1762–1844
CHRISTIAN BROTHER

Rice was born on 1 June 1762 at Westcourt, near Callan, Co Kilkenny. His father was an unusually prosperous Roman Catholic farmer, and after early tuition from an Augustinian friar Edmund was sent at fourteen to complete his education in Kilkenny. At sixteen, he was apprenticed to his uncle, a merchant and ships' chandler in Waterford. He married in his twenties, but his wife died in 1789. Always a devout Catholic, Rice now devoted more and more time and thought to his faith.

A capable businessman, he first managed his uncle's business and then inherited it in 1794. Drawn into charitable works, he helped to house the destitute and alleviate prison conditions, but became increasingly concerned about impoverished boys. In 1802, abandoning an intention to enter an Augustinian monastery in Rome, he opened a boys' school in a stable in New Street, Waterford. He soon retired from business and, joined by two young volunteers from Callan, lived austerely in a loft.

Rice next built a monastery, Mount Sion, on the outskirts of Waterford, setting up a bake-house to feed his hungry pupils. Additional schools were opened at nearby Carrick-on-Suir in 1806 and Dungarvan in 1808. Rice and his companions followed rules adapted from the Presentation nuns and, when they assumed monks' dress, he became Brother Ignatius.

New schools were opened in Cork, Dublin and elsewhere, and in 1817 Rice sought papal approval for a constitution under which all the foundations would be amalgamated under a superior-general. Not all the Catholic bishops welcomed this, but Rice's brother John, rector of the Augustinian college in Rome, gave influential support and in 1822 Brother Ignatius was elected superior-general of the Irish Christian Brothers. The brothers were to devote their lives to the free religious and literary instruction of boys, especially the poor, and were bound by vows of obedience, chastity, poverty and perseverance. Some of Rice's followers chose to continue as Presentation Brothers in Cork; some years later, they too became a papal congregation.

The Christian Brothers' schools soon had a high reputation, and in 1828 the headquarters moved to Dublin. The first English school was opened at Preston in 1825, and others soon followed at Manchester, London, Sunderland and Liverpool. When Rice retired in 1838, the order had seventeen houses and forty-three schools, and this remarkable institution spread to many parts of the world. Rice died at Mount Sion on 29 August 1844.

Visit Rice's home, near Callan, has been carefully restored; nearby are a memorial chapel and monastery. He is interred in a mausoleum at Mount Sion, Waterford, where there is also a memorial chapel.

See Statue of Rice by Peter Grant in Main St, Callan.
Read Desmond Rushe, *Edmund Rice: The Man and His Times* (Gill & Macmillan, Dublin, 1982).

(See plate 7)

—31—
THEOBALD WOLFE TONE
1763–1798
FATHER OF REPUBLICANISM

Tone was born at 44 Stafford Street (now Wolfe Tone Street), Dublin, on 20 June 1763. His father was a Protestant coachmaker who, failing in business, returned to the family farm at Bodenstown, Co Kildare. Tone wanted to become a soldier, but his father insisted he enter Trinity College in 1781. In 1785, he eloped with fifteen-year-old Matilda Witterington; on graduating in 1786, he studied at the Middle Temple in London, and was called to the Irish Bar in 1789.

More interested in politics, Tone published pamphlets critical of the government; an early friend was Thomas Russell, a young army officer returned from India. In 1791 Russell, now stationed in Ulster, asked Tone to draft resolutions for a Bastille day celebration by the Belfast Volunteers. Tone next published *An Argument on behalf of the Catholics of Ireland* under the pseudonym 'A Northern Whig', and was invited to Belfast to assist in founding the Society of United Irishmen. He drafted the manifesto adopted at the inaugural meeting on 18 October 1791.

Tone, generally considered the father of Irish republicanism, was later to write 'To subvert the tyranny of our execrable government, to break the connection with England, the never-failing source of all our political evils, and to assert the independence of my country, these were my objects. To unite the whole people of Ireland, to abolish the memory of past dissensions, and to substitute the common name of Irishman, in place of the denominations of Protestant, Catholic and Dissenter, these were

Lord Edward Fitzgerald, painted by Hugh Douglas Hamilton

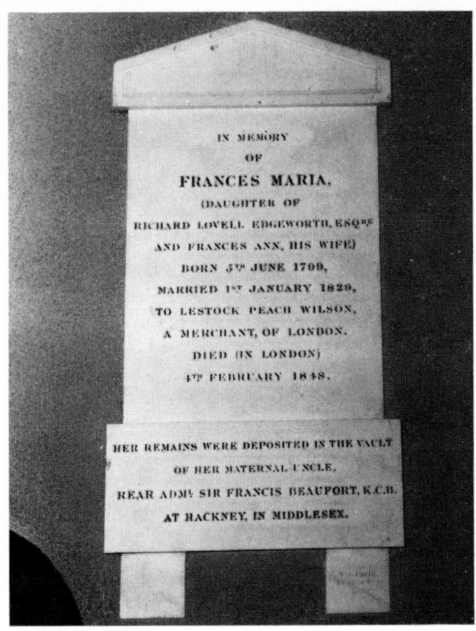

10 Memorial in St John's Church, Edgeworthstown, Co Longford, which has many mementoes of Maria Edgeworth and her family

11 Derrynane House, home of Daniel O'Connell, near Caherdaniel, Co Kerry

12 Statue of Robert Emmet by Jerome Connor, in St Stephen's Green, Dublin

13 Thomas Moore, painted by Willia
Essex

14 George Petrie, painted by Bernard Mulrenin

15 William Carleton, painted by Joh
Slattery

my means.' Initially, the United Irishmen were reformers rather than revolutionaries, and not until 1794 were they forced to become a secret society. A Dublin society was soon formed, but Tone was associated more with the Catholic Committee, whose paid agent he became in 1792. He organised a successful Catholic convention, the 'Back Lane Parliament' held in the Tailors' Hall, and accompanied a delegation which petitioned George III in London. However, the Catholic Relief Act of 1793 disappointed him in not permitting Catholics to sit in parliament.

In 1794, an eccentric Anglican cleric, William Jackson, arrived in Ireland to assess for the French government the likely success of an invasion. Tone unwisely wrote a memorandum suggesting an invasion could succeed with 10,000 troops. When Jackson was betrayed and arrested soon afterwards, Tone had to invoke influential friends to avoid arrest and be allowed to emigrate to America. In 1795, he travelled with his family to Belfast; before sailing for America, he joined other United Irishmen in an oath 'never to desist in our efforts until we had subverted the authority of England over our country, and asserted our independence'. The French minister in Philadelphia encouraged Tone to take his invasion plan to revolutionary France; after some equivocation, the French Directory authorised an expedition under Gen Hoche. The invasion fleet left Brest in December 1796, but through misfortunes at sea the proposed landing in Bantry Bay, Co Cork, was never made.

Tone returned to Paris, and eventually persuaded the French into new expeditions. However, by the time Gen Humbert landed at Killala Bay, Co Mayo, in August 1798 the United Irishmen's rising in Leinster and Ulster had been defeated. Humbert gathered local support, but surrendered in September when Gen Hardy's supporting force failed to arrive. Tone had sailed with Hardy, and after a battle with an English fleet was taken prisoner in Lough Swilly, Co Donegal, on 12 October. Wearing the uniform of a French colonel, he admitted charges of treason at a Dublin court-martial and asked to be shot as a soldier. When his request was refused, he cut his own throat on 12 November, dying in prison on 19 November 1798.

Visit Kilmainham Jail museum, Dublin (open Sun afternoons).
See A plaque marks the site of Tone's home in Wolfe Tone St,

Dublin. Memorial by Edward Delaney in St Stephen's Green, Dublin. He is buried at Bodenstown (1 mile/1.5 km N of Kill, Co Kildare), where a republican memorial has been erected.
Read Frank MacDermot, *Theobald Wolfe Tone and His Times* (Macmillan, 1939; Anvil Books, Dublin, 1968); Henry Boylan, *Theobald Wolfe Tone* (Gill & Macmillan, Dublin, 1981).

(See plate 8)

—32—
LORD EDWARD FITZGERALD
1763–1798
UNITED IRISHMAN

Fitzgerald was born on 15 October 1763. He was the twelfth child of James Fitzgerald, 20th Earl of Kildare, and his wife, daughter of the Duke of Richmond. The earl, whose seat was Carton, Maynooth, Co Kildare, became 1st Duke of Leinster in 1766, but died in 1773. A year later, his widow married William Ogilvie, their sons' Scottish tutor; her brother, now Duke of Richmond, lent them a house at Aubigny in France, where they lived until 1779. Returning to England, Fitzgerald joined the Sussex militia, then served with the 96th infantry in Ireland before being posted to America, where he was wounded at Eutaw Springs in 1781.

After a period in St Lucia, Fitzgerald returned to Ireland in 1783 to become MP for Athy, Co Kildare, supporting Henry Grattan (*qv*) in the Irish parliament. Unsuccessful romances then led him back into the army, and in 1788 he joined the 54th regiment in New Brunswick, where he read Rousseau's *Social Contract* and admired the egalitarian self-sufficiency of Canadians. In 1789, he journeyed to Quebec, then to Detroit, where he was adopted into the Bear tribe of Indians, and finally down the Mississippi river to New Orleans. Returning to England, he had an affair with the dying wife of Richard Brinsley Sheridan (*qv*).

Fitzgerald was friendly with Thomas Paine, author of *Rights of Man*, and in 1792 joined him in Paris. Attending a dinner to celebrate French victories, Fitzgerald toasted the 'speedy abolition of all hereditary titles and feudal distinctions', and was consequently cashiered from the army. He also met and married Pamela Sims, adopted daughter of the novelist and educationalist Madame de Genlis and probably her daughter by the Duke of Orleans. Back in Ireland, Fitzgerald shocked parliament by opining that 'the lord lieutenant and the majority of this House are the worst subjects the King has'.

Fitzgerald increasingly and perhaps recklessly identified himself with the cause of Irish independence; he wore a green cravat, burned turf rather than English coal, and sang patriotic ballads. Early in 1796, he joined the United Irishmen, and in May went to the Continent with a fellow MP, Arthur O'Connor, to discuss with Gen Hoche the possibility of a French invasion. He decided not to contest the 1797 election, telling voters that free elections were impossible under martial law. In January 1798, Fitzgerald headed a military committee to plan the imminent rising; for the United Irishmen he had clear military qualifications to command the insurgents, and it would not be the first time a popular Geraldine had led the Irish.

On 12 March 1798, the members of the Leinster Directory were arrested. Fitzgerald was warned in time and went into hiding; he continued to plan the rising, but was betrayed after the authorities offered a £1,000 reward. He was arrested on 19 May at a house in Thomas Street, Dublin, killing a militia officer in the struggle and himself being shot in the right shoulder by Major Charles Sirr. The weeks of pursuit had also impaired Fitzgerald's health, and on 4 June 1798 he died at Newgate prison, Dublin. He was buried at night in St Werburgh's Church.

See A plaque in Thomas St, Dublin, marks where Fitzgerald was arrested.
Read Patrick Byrne, *Lord Edward Fitzgerald* (Staples Press, 1955).

(See plate 9)

—33— BUCK WHALEY

1766–1800 A RAKE'S PROGRESS

Thomas Whaley was the son of Richard Chapell Whaley, a Protestant landowner and magistrate whose anti-Catholicism earned him the nickname 'Burn-Chapel' Whaley. When the latter died, his son inherited an estate in Co Wicklow, a town house at 86 St Stephen's Green, Dublin, some £60,000 in cash and an income of £7,000 a year. At sixteen, Whaley was sent to Paris, but his tutor was unable to curb the youth's profligacy. After incurring gambling debts of £14,000 in an evening, Whaley had to leave France when his bankers refused to honour his cheque.

Back in Dublin, he was asked one evening in 1788 where he next intended to visit. Having already been nicknamed 'Buck', he was soon to acquire the other name by which he was often known, for he casually replied 'Jerusalem'. His fellow bucks wagered £15,000 that he would not reach the holy city and return within two years. Despite fears of banditry, Whaley immediately launched an expedition to the Holy Land, returning in June 1789 with a signed certificate from a convent in Jerusalem. To win another wager, he had to jump from his drawing room window into the first passing carriage and kiss its occupant; legend places the deed in Dublin, though his memoirs suggest Dover. He also conceived a plan to rescue Louis XVI from the guillotine, but took fright in Paris.

A man of erratic impulses, Whaley unsuccessfully proposed marriage to a young Belfast woman who stood admiring his house; a mistress bore him several children, and on her death he married Lord Cloncurry's daughter in January 1800. He represented Newcastle, Co Dublin, in the Irish parliament from 1785 to 1790, and Enniscorthy, Co Wexford, from 1797 to 1800. Although he took substantial bribes first to vote for the Union with Great Britain and then to vote against it, his financial difficulties forced him to flee to the Isle of Man. To live on Irish soil without being in Ireland (for a bet), he imported earth for the foundations of a new house.

Buck Whaley died of rheumatic fever at Knutsford, Cheshire, on 2 November 1800 while on his way to London. In his last years, he had written his memoirs as a warning to others, but his executors suppressed them and they were not published until 1906.

See Whaley's Dublin home was purchased for the new Catholic University in 1853, and is now occupied by University College, Dublin.

—34— MARIA EDGEWORTH

1767–1849 LITERARY LADY

Maria Edgeworth was born at Black Bourton, Oxfordshire. The date is generally given as 1 January 1767, but may have been a year later. She spent most of her childhood in England before travelling to Edgeworthstown, Co Longford, with her father in 1782. Richard Lovell Edgeworth was not merely a progressive landlord; his many inventions included a telegraph, a velocipede, a land-measuring 'perambulator' and a turnip-cutter. He soon invoked Maria's assistance in managing the family estate and educating the other children of his four marriages; her first publication, *Letters for Literary Ladies* (1795), owed much to his ideas on the education of women. *The Parent's Assistant*, a collection of children's stories, followed in 1796, and she collaborated with her father on *Practical Education* (1798).

Her first novel, *Castle Rackrent* (1800), was an immediate success; it was first published anonymously, but her name appeared on succeeding editions. The book, recounting the history of the dissolute Rackrent family through the voice of their Irish steward, has been described as the first regional novel in English. Her friend, Sir Walter Scott, hoped in his historical novel, *Waverley* (1814), to 'emulate the admirable Irish portraits', and French and Russian novelists owed her a debt.

A second novel, *Belinda*, followed in 1801, and she joined with her father in *Essay on Irish Bulls* (1802), a collection of sometimes inadvertent humour. The two authors visited Paris in 1802, and not without regret Maria turned down a marriage proposal from a Swedish count. Her output was prolific, and she prospered from such novels as *Leonora* (1806), *Tales of Fashionable Life* (1809–12) and *Ormond* (1817), to the last of which her father contributed shortly before his death. Maria completed her father's memoirs, which were published in 1820.

An eye weakness made Maria curtail her reading, writing and needlework for two years, and in 1826 she had to take over management of the estate from her debt-ridden brother Lovell. None the less, she continued to enjoy the prestige of a successful author, and published another novel, *Helen*, in 1834. Throughout her life, Maria revelled in the companionship of a large and eventually scattered family. Her closest friend was her stepmother, Frances Edgeworth, in whose arms she died at Edgeworthstown on 22 May 1849.

Visit St John's Church in Edgeworthstown (or Mostrim); memorabilia include Maria's Sunday purse and a table given by Scott, while the family vault is in the churchyard. There is a small museum on the Athlone road. Edgeworthstown House, much altered, is now a nursing home.
Read Marilyn Butler, *Maria Edgeworth: A Literary Biography* (Oxford University Press, 1972); The World Classics edition of *Castle Rackrent* (OUP, 1980) has a useful introduction by George Watson.

(See plate 10)

—35—
ROBERT STEWART
VISCOUNT CASTLEREAGH
1769–1822
THE MAN BEHIND THE MASK

Stewart was born at 28 Henry Street, Dublin, on 18 June 1769. His father was a Presbyterian landowner, who built an imposing home, Mount Stewart, near Newtownards, Co Down; he supported Henry Grattan (*qv*) in the Irish Parliament. His mother was daughter of a lord lieutenant; his stepmother was daughter of the 1st Earl Camden, a former lord chancellor of England. Educated at Armagh Royal School and St John's College, Cambridge, Stewart was himself elected to the Irish Parliament in 1790.

Although a member of the Northern Whig Club, Stewart leaned instinctively towards William Pitt's Tories and a career at Westminster. In 1794, he married Lady Emily Hobart, daughter of the 2nd Earl of Buckinghamshire, and with Pitt's approval became MP for Tregony in Cornwall. After Pitt recalled the reforming lord lieutenant, Earl Fitzwilliam, in 1795, Stewart's step-uncle, the 2nd Earl Camden, became lord lieutenant.

Stewart gave up his Westminster seat in 1796 and in 1797 joined the Dublin administration. His father was now 1st Earl of Londonderry, and the son became known by the courtesy title of Viscount Castlereagh. In March 1798, Castlereagh became temporary chief secretary in the absence through illness of Thomas Pelham; his good connections overcame the disadvantage of Irish birth, and he retained the post after Lord Cornwallis replaced Camden. Castlereagh was instrumental in the arrest of the United Irishmen's leaders before the 1798 rising began, and was reviled for the cruelty of its suppression. However, he joined with Cornwallis in urging a general amnesty, which the British Government made less generous than they proposed. His appointment was confirmed in November 1798.

Sharing Pitt's commitment to a legislative union of Great Britain and Ireland, Castlereagh secured the passage of the Act of Union in

Ireland by an unscrupulous mixture of bribery and patronage. His effigy was burned outside his house in Merrion Street, and he had to protect himself from the Dublin mob with a pistol. The Act came into force on 1 January 1801, and Castlereagh, Cornwallis and Pitt soon resigned over King George III's refusal to countenance Catholic emancipation.

Thereafter, Castlereagh pursued his political career at Westminster, becoming secretary for war in 1805 and foreign secretary in 1812. He played a notable diplomatic role in the defeat of Napoleon and in the 1815 Congress of Vienna, but repressive domestic policies later made him as unpopular in England as he was in Ireland. Always cold and aloof, he became increasingly depressive, and on 12 August 1822 he cut his throat at his country seat in Kent. Historians have treated him more kindly than contemporaries such as Byron, who described him as a man who had cut his country's throat, and Shelley, who wrote:

> I met Murder on the way –
> He had a mask like Castlereagh –
> Very smooth he looked, yet grim;
> Seven bloodhounds followed him.

Visit Mount Stewart (5 miles/8 km SE of Newtownards) is a National Trust property (guidebook). (House open afternoons, April–Sept, except Fri; garden open afternoons, April–Oct.)
Read Wendy Hinde, *Castlereagh* (Collins, 1981).

—36—
EDWARD BUNTING

1773–1843
A MAN OF AIRS

Bunting was born in Armagh in 1773. His father, a Derbyshire engineer employed at Dungannon colliery, died soon afterwards; his mother was Irish. Bunting was the youngest of three sons, all of whom became musicians. The eldest, an organist at Drogheda, Co Louth, was Edward's first teacher. At eleven, Edward was sent to

Belfast, being articled to the organist of St Anne's Church. A musical prodigy, he quickly became popular as performer and teacher.

Bunting lived with a Presbyterian family, the McCrackens, who were much influenced by revolutionary ideas from America and France; the son, Henry Joy McCracken, was hanged as a United Irishman in 1798. An ambitious harpers' festival was held in Belfast in July 1792, coinciding with celebrations commemorating the storming of the Bastille in Paris. The harpers performed over three days; all but one were old, and a majority were blind. One of the promoters was Henry Joy, a newspaper proprietor and uncle of Henry Joy McCracken, and Bunting was commissioned to transcribe the music. His imagination was immediately stirred, and he soon set off with the harper Denis Hempson to collect airs in the Magilligan district of Co Londonderry. When Bunting played an Irish air, 'The Parting of Comrades', at a farewell party for Wolfe Tone (*qv*) in 1795, Tone's wife was reduced to tears.

In 1796, his pioneering work was published as *A General Collection of the Ancient Irish Music*, which included sixty-six airs adapted for the pianoforte. In 1802, Bunting made an extended tour of Connacht and Munster, but now collected the verses accompanying airs. Not knowing Irish, he was assisted by Patrick Lynch, a Co Down schoolmaster. In 1809, he published a second volume, containing seventy-seven airs, of which twenty had verses translated from the Irish; the English words had no great merit, but the original notebooks of Bunting and Lynch have been preserved. A year earlier, Thomas Moore (*qv*) had drawn from the 1796 volume the music for eleven of his *Irish Melodies*.

On the formation of the Belfast Harp Society in 1808, Bunting became its musical director; in 1813, he staged a music festival. In 1815, he toured Europe extensively, playing Irish music to appreciative audiences. In 1819, he married and became organist of St George's Church in Hardwicke Place, Dublin. George Petrie (*qv*) encouraged him to publish his third volume, *The Ancient Music of Ireland* (1840), contributing an informative essay on the Irish harp and harpers. Bunting died in Dublin on 21 December 1843, and was buried in Mount Jerome Cemetery.

—37—
DANIEL O'CONNELL

1775–1847
'THE LIBERATOR'

O'Connell was born at Carhan House, near Cahirciveen, Co Kerry, on 6 August 1775. His father was a small landowner, and the boy was soon adopted by his childless uncle, Maurice 'Hunting Cap' O'Connell, of Derrynane House, overlooking Kenmare Bay. After early schooling in Cobh, Co Cork, he attended English colleges in St Omer and Douai in 1791–3, but had to flee France when revolutionaries closed them. The O'Connells were prosperous Roman Catholics, on good terms with the local Protestant ascendancy; although it had been illegal to educate the boy abroad, this was changed by a 1792 Relief Act, which also made it possible for him to become a barrister.

After studying at Lincoln's Inn, London, O'Connell was called to the Irish Bar in 1798 and practised with great industry and success on the Munster circuit. In 1802, he married his cousin from Tralee, Mary O'Connell. Innately conservative in politics, O'Connell opposed the violence of the 1798 and 1803 risings – 'no political change whatsoever is worth the shedding of a single drop of human blood' – and in 1815 he was much distressed when he killed a member of Dublin Corporation who had forced him into a duel.

In his first public speech, in 1800, O'Connell opposed the Union with Great Britain. Its repeal became one of his great political objectives; the other was Catholic emancipation, opening up state and judicial appointments and the right to sit in parliament. In 1823, he founded the Catholic Association; membership, initially costing a guinea a year, was widened to embrace those who could afford a 'Catholic rent' of a penny a month. A powerful nationwide organisation quickly emerged, with the help of the clergy, and in 1824 the government unsuccessfully prosecuted O'Connell for inciting rebellion. When in 1825 a Bill was introduced to suppress the Association, O'Connell formed a new one.

In the 1826 general election, the Association organised the 'forty shilling freeholders' to elect a number of MPs sympathetic to emancipation. In 1828, O'Connell himself won a by-election in Co Clare, though his unwillingness to take the anti-Catholic oath of supremacy prevented him from taking his seat at Westminster. It was to protect the forty shilling freeholders that O'Connell had founded in 1826 his Order of Liberators; hitherto known as 'The Counsellor', he now became 'The Liberator'. In 1829, the government conceded Catholic emancipation, though raising the electoral qualification from 40s to £10, and after a further by-election O'Connell entered parliament.

In 1835, O'Connell's supporters at Westminster held a balance of power between Whigs and Tories, and he negotiated the informal 'Lichfield House compact' with the Whigs, leading to four years of enlightened administration, attributed to the Dublin Castle under-secretary, Thomas Drummond. In 1840, O'Connell again marshalled mass support in the National Repeal Association. In March 1843, he addressed the first of a series of 'monster rallies' at Trim, Co Meath. Such was O'Connell's oratory that, in August, he drew an estimated audience of three-quarters of a million to the Hill of Tara, Co Meath.

A final rally was planned for Clontarf, on the outskirts of Dublin, on 8 October 1843, but the government banned it and stationed troops at the approaches. O'Connell, ever the constitutionalist, cancelled the meeting. He soon faced charges of creating discontent and disaffection among the Queen's subjects, and was found guilty in February 1844. The House of Lords reversed the judgement, but O'Connell's health had declined during three months' imprisonment and he had lost ground to the more militant 'Young Ireland' movement led by Thomas Davis (*qv*). His last Commons appearance was on 8 February 1847, when he appealed to MPs to save Ireland, now gripped by the potato famine: 'If you don't save her, she cannot save herself.' Accepting medical advice, he set out for Rome, but died in Genoa on 15 May 1847. His heart was embalmed and taken to Rome; his body was returned to Ireland.

Visit Derrynane House and grounds (1½ miles/2 km SW of Caherdaniel, Co Kerry), now a national historic park and museum (guidebook; open throughout the year).
See Ruins of Carhan House (1 mile/1.5 km ENE of Cahirciveen). Statues by James Cahill in O'Connell Sq, Ennis, Co Clare, by John

Hogan in the Crescent, Limerick, and by John Henry Foley in O'Connell St, Dublin. A plaque marks O'Connell's Dublin home at 58 Merrion Square. Grave and round tower memorial in Glasnevin cemetery, Dublin.

Read Seán O'Faoláin, *King of the Beggars* (Nelson, 1938; Allen Figgis, Dublin, 1970). R. Dudley Edwards, *Daniel O'Connell and his world* (Thames & Hudson, 1975).

(See plate 11)

—38—
ROBERT EMMET
1778–1803
YOUNG HERO

Emmet was born at 124 St Stephen's Green, Dublin, on 4 March 1778. He was the youngest son of Dr Robert Emmet, physician to the lord lieutenant, and brother of the United Irishman Thomas Addis Emmet. He entered Trinity College in 1793, joined the United Irishmen soon afterwards, and was consequently expelled from college in February 1798.

Thomas Addis Emmet was arrested in March 1798, and, after the failure of the subsequent rising, consented to exile. He was first confined at Fort George in Scotland; released in 1802, he lived in Paris before emigrating to America in 1804. Meanwhile, Robert had become a wanted man in Ireland, and travelled extensively among Irish refugees in Europe. He sought his brother's advice about a new rising, and met the French leaders, Bonaparte and Talleyrand; doubting the sincerity of Bonaparte's professed support for Irish independence, Emmet returned to Dublin in October 1802 to plan a rising without French aid. However, he had also met Thomas Russell, friend of Wolfe Tone (*qv*) and recently released from Fort George; Russell undertook to lead the rising in Ulster.

Moving around Dublin at night or in disguise, Emmet managed to establish arms depots, and with Russell tested an explosive rocket at Rathfarnham. On the evening of 23 July 1803, he donned a green uniform and cocked hat, and led a hundred followers towards

Dublin Castle. On their way, they stopped the carriage of the Lord Chief Justice, Lord Kilwarden, and murdered him and his nephew. The rabble were quickly dispersed, however, and Emmet fled to the Wicklow mountains. No Ulster rising occurred.

His love of Sarah Curran, daughter of John Philpot Curran (*qv*), kept him from escaping to France. He was discovered in a hiding place at Harold's Cross, and arrested by Major Sirr, the captor of Lord Edward Fitzgerald (*qv*). The fiasco of Emmet's rising was redeemed by his subsequent speech from the dock, ending with the famous words 'Let no man write my epitaph; for as no man who knows my motives dare now vindicate them, let not prejudice or ignorance asperse them. Let them and me rest in obscurity and peace, and my tomb remain uninscribed, and my memory in oblivion, until other times and other men can do justice to my character. When my country takes her place among the nations of the earth, then, and not till then, let my epitaph be written. I have done.'

On 20 September 1803, Emmet was hanged in Thomas Street, Dublin. Russell was betrayed to Sirr and hanged at Downpatrick, Co Down, on 21 October 1803, prompting Florence M. Wilson's poem 'The Man from God Knows Where'. Emmet's death inspired his college friend Thomas Moore (*qv*) to write 'O breathe not his name' and, recalling his romance with Sarah Curran, 'She is far from the land where her young hero sleeps.'

See A statue of Emmet by Jerome Connor faces his birthplace in St Stephen's Green, Dublin.

Read Leon Ó Broin, *The Unfortunate Mr. Robert Emmet* (Clonmore & Reynolds, Dublin, 1958; Burns Oates & Washbourne, 1958).

(See plate 12)

—39—
THOMAS MOORE
1779–1852
THE MINSTREL BOY

Moore was born on 28 May 1779 at 12 Aungier Street, Dublin, where his father had a prosperous spirit grocery. At an early age, he displayed gifts as an actor and mimic, and these were encouraged at Samuel Whyte's academy in Grafton Street. An easing of the penal laws against Roman Catholics in 1793 allowed Moore's ambitious mother to plan a legal career for her son, and in 1794 he entered Trinity College, Dublin. One of his closest friends was Robert Emmet (*qv*), but he managed not to become embroiled with the United Irishmen, though he shared their ideals. Another college friend, Edward Hudson, awakened Moore's interest in Irish music, and both young men were deeply moved by the first collection of Irish airs published by Edward Bunting (*qv*) in 1796. Moore's principal achievement at Trinity College, Dublin, however, was a translation of the *Odes of Anacreon*.

Graduating in 1798, Moore entered the Middle Temple in London the following year. Irish friends introduced him to London society, and he was an immediate success, enjoying the patronage of Lord Moira; his playing and singing opened the great houses to him, and when *Anacreon* was published in 1800 he was able to dedicate it to the Prince Regent. In 1803, Moore turned down the offer of a new poet laureateship of Ireland, and through Lord Moira's influence became admiralty registrar in Bermuda; he found the post uncongenial and, appointing a deputy, returned to London. In 1808, he published his first volume of *Irish Melodies*, with music by Sir John Stevenson; the tenth and last appeared in 1834. Many of the melodies, such as 'The last rose of summer' and 'Believe me if all those endearing young charms', were love songs; others, such as 'The harp that once' and 'The minstrel boy', were stirring patriotic ballads as acceptable to the English as to the Irish.

Moore had a regular income from the melodies, in return for his willingness to perform them. Other writings, including satires such as *Corruption and Intolerance* (1808) and *The Sceptic* (1809) and a comic opera, *M.P. or The Blue Stocking* (1811), proved less enduring. So did his long, oriental poem, *Lalla Rookh*, though it went into its seventh edition less than a year after publication in 1817. In 1811, Moore married Bessy Dyke, with whom he had acted in Richard Power's private theatre in Kilkenny; it was a happy union, save that their five children predeceased them. There were recurrent financial problems, often the consequence of Moore's own pride and high principles, and in 1819 he fled to France to escape a debtor's prison after his deputy in Bermuda had stolen £6,000. Not until 1822 was he able to settle again in England. While abroad, he was entrusted with Lord Byron's memoirs, but after the poet's death in 1824 he reluctantly allowed Byron's half-sister to destroy them for fear publication would cause a scandal; Moore published his own biography of Byron in 1830. His later writings also included biographies of Richard Brinsley Sheridan (1825) and Lord Edward Fitzgerald (1831) (*qqv*), and an unusual patriotic novel-cum-history, *Memoirs of Captain Rock* (1824). He spent his latter years in the village of Sloperton, in Wiltshire, where he died on 25 February 1852.

See Statue by Christopher Moore at the junction of Westmoreland St and College St, Dublin. A plaque marks Moore's birthplace.
Read Terence de Vere White, *Tom Moore* (Hamish Hamilton, 1977); David Hammond (ed), *Moore's Melodies* (Gilbert Dalton, Skerries, Co Dublin, 1979), a bicentenary selection with extracts from the poet's memoirs, journals and correspondence.

(See plate 13)

—40— CHARLES BIANCONI

1786–1875
KING OF THE ROADS

Carlo Bianconi was born in northern Italy on 24 September 1786. His father owned a modest farm and silk mill, and the boy was originally destined for the priesthood. He showed neither vocation nor scholarship, however, and at fifteen (to end a youthful romance) he was apprenticed to an Italian print-maker who took him to Dublin. Young Charles – as he called himself, though his English was imperfect – was soon tramping the roads to Waterford and Wexford to sell prints, and continued on his own account after his apprenticeship ended in 1804. An early friend was Theobald Matthew (*qv*), who rescued him from a fight, and in Waterford Edmund Rice (*qv*) helped him improve his education. In 1809, Bianconi opened a shop in Clonmel, Co Tipperary, selling prints and mirrors; soon he was dealing very profitably in gold bullion, reselling peasants' guineas to the government for the Napoleonic wars.

When peace brought a fall in the demand for horses and in grain prices, Bianconi saw an opportunity to provide cheaper and better public transport than was available by stagecoach or waterway. He negotiated a contract to carry mail, and on 6 July 1815 the first Bianconi car (a horse-drawn two-wheeler carrying six passengers back to back facing the roadside) travelled ten miles from Clonmel to Cahir, Co Tipperary. Within a year, 'Bians' were covering more than 200 miles a day, in a network extending from Limerick to Waterford. Within twenty years, the crimson and yellow open cars were (in different sizes) a familiar sight almost everywhere west of a line joining Letterkenny, Co Donegal, and Wexford.

As a young man, Bianconi had met Daniel O'Connell (*qv*), and he was an early member of O'Connell's Catholic Association. He became a popular figure among Irish Catholics when, in 1826, Bians were used to bring O'Connell's supporters to vote in a critical Waterford by-election. Later, he joined O'Connell's Order of

16 Telescope constructed by William Parsons, 3rd Earl of Rosse, in Birr Castle, Co Offaly

17 John O'Donovan, painted by Charles Grey

18 Avondale, home of Charles Stewart Parnell, near Rathdrum, Co Wicklow

19 The 'autograph' tree at Coole Park, home of Lady Gregory, near Gort, Co Galway. Initials include those of J. M. Synge (top right), George Bernard Shaw (below Synge), Augusta Gregory (left of GBS), Violet Martin ('Martin Ross', further left), George Russell ('AE', in triangle) and (to the right of AE) W. B. Yeats and Seán O'Casey

20 Edward Carson, Baron Carson of Duncairn, painted by Frank McKelvey

21 Douglas Hyde, painted by Seán O'Sullivan

22 Roger Casement, painted by Sarah Purser

23 Thoor Ballylee, home of W. B. Yeats, near Gort, Co Galway

Liberators. In 1827, he married Eliza Hayes, the young daughter of a Dublin stockbroker. Eliza proved a proficient hostess for her increasingly influential husband, but his heart was always with his first Italian love.

Bianconi became a naturalised British subject in 1831, which allowed him to buy land. He entertained many notables at Silver Spring, his new home outside Clonmel, and in 1844 became mayor of the town. In 1846, he bought Longfield, an imposing house near Cashel, Co Tipperary, which he had coveted since his peddling days, and proved a beneficent landlord during the famine years. In 1863, he became a deputy lieutenant for the county.

When, in 1843, Bianconi addressed a meeting in Cork of the British Association for the Advancement of Science, his cars were covering almost 4,000 miles a day. Already railways were being built, and the farsighted businessman refused to join canal-owners in resisting the new; instead, he bought shares in railway companies, and re-routed his Bians to connect with rail services. A driving accident in 1865 persuaded him to begin selling his coaching empire, usually on generous terms to his agents and employees. He died at Longfield on 22 September 1875.

Read M. O'C. Bianconi & S. J. Watson, *Bianconi: King of the Irish Roads* (Allen Figgis, Dublin, 1962).

—41—
HENRY COOKE
1788–1868
'THE BLACK MAN'

Cooke was born at Grillagh, near Maghera, Co Derry, on 11 May 1788. The son of a tenant farmer, he was educated locally before entering Glasgow College in 1802. Academically undistinguished, he took pains to become a forceful public speaker, and was ordained a Presbyterian minister in 1808. He served first in Co Antrim at Duneane, near Randalstown, and then at Donegore. He married in 1813, and his presbytery allowed him to study further at Glasgow and at Trinity College and the Royal College of Surgeons, Dublin.

In 1818, he was called to Killyleagh, Co Down.

More than anyone, Cooke led Ulster Presbyterianism away from the free-thinking radicalism which had spawned the United Irishmen's rising during his childhood. He gained prominence in 1821 by routing in debate a visiting English preacher, John Smethurst, who held Arian or Unitarian views. In 1824, he was elected moderator of the Synod of Ulster. By 1829, his oratorical command over the synod was such that the Arians, led by his rival Henry Montgomery, were forced to withdraw. In the same year, he received an American doctorate from Jefferson College and was called to a new church in May Street, Belfast, where he drew large congregations. In 1836, the synod made subscription to the Westminster Confession of Faith obligatory, and in 1840 it merged with the even more conservative Secession Synod to form the General Assembly of the Presbyterian Church in Ireland. Cooke was elected moderator in 1841 and again in 1862.

In defeating the Arians, Cooke had deliberately expelled political liberals; Montgomery's elder brothers had fought as United Irishmen. In 1834, Cooke addressed a mass rally of Protestants at Hillsborough, Co Down, forging a new alliance between Presbyterians and the established Church of Ireland to defend their interests against the newly emancipated Catholics. When Daniel O'Connell (*qv*) visited Belfast in 1841, Cooke staged a huge anti-Repeal rally. So close was he to the Anglican landed aristocracy that, when in 1843 the General Assembly sought to have more Presbyterian MPs, Cooke withdrew until the policy was rescinded in 1847.

He opposed the national system of undenominational schooling begun in 1831, and in 1840 won financial aid for Presbyterian schools. He also secured government support for a new Presbyterian College in Belfast, and in 1847 became its president and professor of sacred rhetoric and catechetics. Thereafter, he served the May Street church as unpaid 'constant supplier', finally retiring in 1867. He died in Belfast on 13 December 1868.

See Statue of Cooke, a local landmark known as 'The Black Man', in College Square East, Belfast.
Read Finlay Holmes, *Henry Cooke* (Christian Journals, Belfast, 1981).

—42—
GEORGE PETRIE
1789–1866
A GREAT COLLECTOR

Petrie was born of Scottish stock in Dublin in 1789. His father was a miniaturist who painted many leaders of the 1798 rising. Petrie attended the Dublin Society's art school, and became a professional artist. At nineteen, he made the first of many walking tours, sketching scenery and antiquities in the Wicklow mountains and noting down the songs he heard each evening in wayside cottages. His engravings appeared in popular guidebooks such as Cromwell's *Excursions in Ireland* and Brewster's *Beauties of Ireland*. He married in 1821.

Petrie exhibited landscapes at Somerset House, in London, in 1816, and at the first Royal Hibernian Academy exhibition in 1826. He was elected to the RHA in 1828, becoming its librarian in 1830. He also joined the Royal Irish Academy in 1828, and worked hard to improve its museum and library; in 1831, he bought and presented to the RIA a valuable manuscript of the second part of the *Annals of the Four Masters* (see Mícheál Ó Cléirigh), and among purchases now in the National Museum was the twelfth-century Cross of Cong. In 1832–3, he helped to run *The Dublin Penny Journal*, contributing articles and drawings on antiquities; it lasted a year, as did *The Irish Penny Journal*, which Petrie edited in 1840–1.

In 1833, Petrie joined the young Ordnance Survey of Ireland. With the help of scholars such as John O'Donovan (*qv*) and Eugene O'Curry, and of the poet James Clarence Mangan, he compiled data for memoirs to accompany the county maps; for financial reasons, only one memoir appeared, but the work gave great impetus to Irish studies. Petrie's important archaeological writings included 'On the Origin and Uses of the Round Towers of Ireland' (1833), which was embodied in *The Ecclesiastical Architecture of Ireland* (1845), and 'On the History and Antiquities of Tara Hill' (1839).

His association with the Ordnance Survey ended in 1846, but in 1849 a government pension helped him to carry on his researches. Petrie believed that, following the potato famine of 1845–9, innumerable melodies could disappear forever, and in 1851 he helped to found the Society for the Preservation and Publication of the Melodies of Ireland. In 1855, the society published *The Petrie Collection of the Ancient Music of Ireland*, with exhaustive notes on its 147 airs and generally more authoritative than his friend Edward Bunting (*qv*) had been; an unnamed air was to become famous as 'The Londonderry Air'. A second, incomplete volume was published in 1882, and Sir Charles Stanford (*qv*) published 1,582 airs in *The Complete Collection of Irish Music as Noted by George Petrie* in 1902–5. Petrie died in Dublin on 17 January 1866, and was buried at Mount Jerome cemetery.

See A plaque marks Petrie's home at 21 Great Charles St, Dublin.
Read Grace J. Calder, *George Petrie & The Ancient Music of Ireland* (Dolmen Press, Dublin, 1968).

(See plate 14)

—43—
FATHER THEOBALD MATHEW
1790–1856
APOSTLE OF TEMPERANCE

Mathew was born at Thomastown Castle, near Golden, Co Tipperary, on 10 October 1790. His Roman Catholic father was land agent to a cousin, the 1st Baron Llandaff, who had discreetly become a Protestant to preserve the family estates. On leaving St Canice's Academy in Kilkenny, Mathew entered Maynooth College in 1807, but left after a breach of the seminary's rules and entered the Capuchin convent at Church Street, Dublin. He was ordained in 1814.

After a brief period in Kilkenny, Father Mathew was sent to the 'Little Friary' in Blackamoor Lane, Cork, where he won a reputation as preacher and sympathetic confessor. He opened a school where girls were taught elementary subjects as well as sewing and housework. In 1819, he founded a society whose young men worked among the poor and the sick and helped him in an evening school for boys. In 1822, Mathew was elected provincial of the Irish Capuchins, holding office until 1851.

Increasingly, Mathew became aware of the evils of alcohol, to which the Catholic poor turned as a relief from their miserable conditions. The first temperance societies directed their efforts against spirits, but in the 1830s there was growing advocacy of total abstinence. Mathew was persuaded to become president of the new Cork Total Abstinence Society, enrolling on 10 April 1838 with the words 'Here goes in the name of the Lord'.

Within five months, the society had over five thousand members, each pledging lifelong abstinence and receiving a medal. Mathew's house in Cove Street attracted a stream of pilgrims, and he was soon in demand all over Ireland, addressing enormous crowds. On a visit to Limerick in 1839, he enrolled 150,000 members in two days. The decline in drunkenness made it possible for Daniel O'Connell (*qv*) to stage peaceful rallies, though the temperance bands were sometimes a noisy nuisance; crime diminished sharply, as did government revenues from spirit duties.

Mathew's generosity outweighed his financial acumen, and he often gave away medals he could have sold; when arrested for debt to a medal manufacturer, he was forced to appeal publicly for funds, and his problems probably prevented him becoming bishop of Cork in 1847. The years of the potato famine brought new stresses, and in 1848 he suffered a stroke. Despite this, he pursued his crusade in America as he had done earlier in Great Britain, and became only the second foreigner allowed to sit on the floor of the US Senate. When he returned to Cork in 1851, the evils of eviction, emigration and starvation had gravely damaged the temperance movement, and Mathew was no longer strong enough to revitalise it. He died in Queenstown (now Cobh), Co Cork, on 8 December 1856, and was buried in St Joseph's cemetery, Cork.

See Statues in Patrick St, Cork; O'Connell St, Dublin; and at Thomastown (1½ miles/2 km W of Golden on the Cashel–Tipperary road), near Thomastown Castle ruins.

Read Patrick Rogers, *Father Theobald Mathew: Apostle of Temperance* (Browne & Nolan, Dublin, 1943).

—44—
WILLIAM CARLETON
1794–1869
PICARESQUE PEASANT

Carleton was born at Prillisk, near Clogher, Co Tyrone, on 20 February 1794. He was the youngest child of a Roman Catholic farmer, who was fluent in English as well as Irish and a storehouse of folklore and antiquarian knowledge. Carleton's family hoped he would enter the priesthood and, after attending a hedge school, he set out for Munster as a 'poor scholar' only to return after an ominous dream. In 1814–16, he attended a classical school in Glaslough, Co Monaghan. Later, a pilgrimage to Lough Derg, Co Donegal, turned his mind against Catholicism.

Fond of dancing and athletic pursuits, Carleton lived an idle life which his family increasingly resented. Happening on the picaresque novel, *Gil Blas*, he set out like its hero to see the world. In a precarious existence, he tutored briefly in Co Louth and ran a hedge school at Newcastle, Co Dublin, before arriving in Dublin in 1818. His money was quickly spent, and he had sight of the city's poverty-stricken underworld before finding work as a tutor. He soon married Jane Anderson, niece of one of his employers.

Carleton began to write fictionalised sketches of his adventures, and in 1825 an account of the Lough Derg pilgrimage was published in *The Christian Examiner*. Its editor, Rev Caesar Otway, welcomed Carleton as a convert from Catholicism, and printed other sketches, which were collected in 1830 as *Traits and Stories of the Irish Peasantry*. A second series followed in 1833, and in 1834 Carleton published *Tales of Ireland*. His first novel was *Fardorougha the Miser* (1839), which Isaac Butt (*qv*) had published in the *Dublin University Magazine*. Later novels included *Valentine M'Clutchy* (1845), on eviction; *Rody the Rover* (1845), on Ribbonmen and other secret societies; *The Black Prophet* (1847), on the potato famine; and *The Emigrants of Ahadarra* (1847).

His shorter works are best, but the novels also contain piercing glimpses of peasant life. Carleton wrote for anyone who would pay, and there is no consistent political view, but his portraits of poor scholar, hedge schoolmaster, matchmaker and others form a rich gallery. However, despite his success, he was always in financial difficulty, even after he secured a civil list pension. His later novels are inferior, but the sentimental *Willy Reilly and His Dear Colleen Bawn* (1855) was enormously popular. He died in Dublin on 30 January, 1869, and was buried in Mount Jerome cemetery.

See At Springtown (2 miles/3 km E of Augher, Co Tyrone), a plaque marks the cottage where Carleton spent his youth.
Read Benedict Kiely, *Poor Scholar: A Study of the Works and Days of William Carleton (1794–1869)* (Sheed & Ward, 1947; Talbot Press, Dublin, 1972).

(See plate 15)

—45—
WILLIAM DARGAN
1799–1867
RAILWAY BUILDER

Dargan, a farmer's son, was born in Co Carlow on 28 February 1799. Educated in England, he was employed in a surveyor's office and worked under Thomas Telford in constructing the Holyhead road in 1820. He returned to Ireland to start his own business, and built the road from Dublin to Howth. In 1831, he began construction of the first railway in Ireland, from Dublin to Kingstown (now Dun Laoghaire), which opened in 1838. By 1853, he had built over six hundred miles of railway, including the Dublin and Drogheda railway, the Great Southern and Western to Cork, and the Midland and Great Western to Galway. One interesting experiment was the 'atmospheric railway' joining Kingstown and Dalkey, Co Dublin, which used compressed air for propulsion.

Several of Dargan's railways were in Ulster, joining Belfast to Bangor, Carrickfergus and Portadown. His Ulster Canal linked Lough Neagh and Lough Erne. He constructed a deep-water harbour at Belfast, creating incidentally Dargan's Island, which was to become the Queen's Island of shipbuilding renown. Dargan operated some railways profitably, as well as being the most successful of Ireland's railway builders, and he became a millionaire.

The Great Exhibition of 1851 in London inspired Dargan to encourage Irish manufacturing and tourism by promoting an industrial exhibition in Dublin. He advanced almost £100,000 to the organising committee, and on 12 May 1853 the exhibition was opened by the lord lieutenant on Leinster Lawn, overlooking Merrion Square and beside the then headquarters of the Royal Dublin Society in Leinster House. The climax of the exhibition was the August visit of Queen Victoria, who called on Dargan and his wife at their palatial mansion at Mount Anville, Dundrum, Co Dublin. She offered him a baronetcy, but he turned it down. Dargan had assembled a number of fine paintings in the temporary exhibition hall, and he now conceived the idea of a national collection. Although he had lost £20,000 on the exhibition, he proceeded to plan the National Gallery, which was built on Leinster Lawn and opened in 1864.

Following the exhibition, Dargan turned his attention to flax-growing, and established mills around Dublin. For once, his business judgement was faulty, and he began to lose money. His principal business interest was now the Dublin, Wicklow and Wexford railway, of which he was chairman. However, he had never been good at delegating work and, after a serious fall from his horse in 1866, his business interests went rapidly into decline. Having sold his Dundrum house, he was close to bankruptcy when he died at his town house, 2 Fitzwilliam Square, on 7 February 1867. He was buried at Glasnevin cemetery.

See Statue by Thomas Farrell in front of the National Gallery, Merrion Sq, Dublin.

—46—
WILLIAM PARSONS
3rd EARL OF ROSSE
1800–1867
ASTRONOMER EXTRAORDINARY

Parsons was born in York, England, on 17 June 1800, but spent most of his life at Birr, Co Offaly, then known as Parsonstown in King's County. Birr Castle had been acquired in 1620 by an adventurous ancestor, Sir Laurence Parsons, from the turbulent O'Carrolls, and it withstood sieges in 1643 and 1690. The 2nd Earl was an enthusiastic member of the 'patriot party' in the Irish parliament, but after the 1800 Acts of Union lost interest in politics. Parsons was taught by his father before going to Trinity College, Dublin, and then to Magdalen College, Oxford, where he took first class honours in mathematics. He became MP for King's County in 1823, but was more interested in science and resigned in 1834. In 1836, he married a Yorkshire heiress, Mary Field, who encouraged his experiments and was herself an early member of the Irish Photographic Society.

Parsons, now Lord Oxmanton, constructed his first telescope on the lawn in front of Birr Castle. Its speculum (the curved, polished metal reflector) was 3ft (0.9m) in diameter. The process for silvering mirrors had not been discovered, and casting brittle specula called for patient experiment. On succeeding to his father's title in 1841, Parsons embarked on constructing a telescope which was until 1917 the largest reflecting telescope in the world. The 6ft (1.8m) reflector was successfully cast in 1843, and two years later it was in place in a tube 56ft (17m) long and 7ft (2.1m) in diameter, which could be raised towards the heavens between two 50ft (15.25m) high walls. Only through the 'leviathan of Birr Castle' could astronomers study the spiral shapes of nebulae, and the Earl's drawings compared favourably with photographs taken many years later.

Rosse became president of the Royal Society from 1848 to 1854, was a member of the Royal Irish Academy, and was chancellor of

Dublin University from 1862 until his death at Monkstown, Co Dublin, on 31 October 1867. His son Laurence also became an eminent astronomer.

Visit Birr Castle demesne, with magnificently diverse gardens (guidebook). The walls and tube of Rosse's telescope remain, and a small museum records his achievements. (The mirror of the telescope is in the Science Museum in South Kensington, London.) Nearby is the early suspension bridge which he designed to span the Camcor river.

(See plate 16)

—47—
SIR WILLIAM ROWAN HAMILTON
1805–1865
MATHEMATICAL GENIUS

Hamilton, a solicitor's son, was born at 36 Lower Dominick Street (now demolished), Dublin, on 4 August 1805. At seven, he could read Hebrew; at twelve, he had a knowledge of Arabic, Hindustani, Malay, Persian and Sanskrit, in addition to commoner languages. These were encouraged with a view to a clerkship in the East India Company, but Hamilton revealed a greater precocity in mathematics, and at seventeen had detected an error of reasoning in Pierre Laplace's classic *Mécanique Céleste*. The Irish astronomer royal, Dr John Brinkley, soon pronounced him 'the first mathematician of his age'.

In 1824, during his second year at Trinity College, Dublin, he read a paper to the Royal Irish Academy, and was encouraged to develop this into a 'Theory of System of Rays' (1828), which on theoretical grounds predicted conical refraction. He was still an undergraduate when in 1827 he was appointed professor of astronomy at Trinity College and astronomer royal at Dunsink observatory, Finglas, Dublin. As secretary to the British Association when it visited Dublin in 1835, he received a knighthood. In

1837, he became president of the Royal Irish Academy, and he was also a corresponding member of the Academy of St Petersburg and first foreign member of the National Academy of Sciences in America.

Hamilton received gold medals from the Royal Society for his work on optics and dynamics. He applied his optical methods to dynamics, making use of a principle of varying action which became known as 'Hamilton's principle'. His later work was in pure mathematics, and in 1844 he defined the 'quaternions' which were to form the basis of his new calculus. His system was detailed in his *Lectures on Quaternions*, begun at Trinity College, Dublin, in 1848 and published in 1853; it had many applications in solid geometry, physics, astronomy, crystallography, electrodynamics and other studies involving motion in three-dimensional space. Hamilton's friend, the Edinburgh mathematician P. G. Tait, compared quaternions to an elephant's trunk, 'ready at any moment to do anything, be it to pick up a crumb or a field gun, to strangle a tiger, or uproot a tree'.

Throughout his life, Hamilton read widely in the many languages at his command. He wrote poetry, and numbered William Wordsworth and Maria Edgeworth (*qv*) among his friends. He was much preoccupied with completing *The Elements of Quaternions* when he died in Dublin on 2 September 1865, and the work was edited for publication in 1866 by his son.

See A plaque on the Royal Canal bridge at Broombridge Rd, Dublin, records the 'flash of genius' by which Hamilton, on 16 October 1843, discovered the formula for quaternion multiplication and scratched it on the stonework with a penknife.

—48—
JOHN O'DONOVAN
1809–1861
GAELIC SCHOLAR

O'Donovan was born on 9 July 1809 at Attateemore, Co Kilkenny. His father was a farmer who, on his deathbed, repeated several times to his son their line of descent from a 3rd century king of Munster. O'Donovan was well educated locally and in Dublin, despite the limited opportunities for Roman Catholics, and in 1826 he joined the Irish Record Office, working on Irish manuscripts and law documents. In 1829, he was appointed to the historical department of the Ordnance Survey of Ireland, initially working on place-names for maps but later, under George Petrie (*qv*), collecting historical material for the proposed memoirs to accompany the maps. His letters were subsequently edited by Father Michael O'Flanagan as *The John O'Donovan Archaeological Survey* (fifty volumes, 1924–32).

During this period, O'Donovan also wrote for *The Dublin Penny Journal* and *The Irish Penny Journal*, notably a valuable series on Irish family names. In 1840, he and his co-worker and brother-in-law Eugene O'Curry helped to found the Irish Archaeological Society, which published much of his best work. O'Donovan also produced a number of original maps of ancient Ireland. He was a prolific scholar, translating many early manuscripts. In 1845, *A Grammar of the Irish Language* compared medieval and modern modes of spoken and written Irish. He wrote a supplement to Edward O'Reilly's *Irish Dictionary*, which was published posthumously.

His greatest work of scholarship was to translate the *Annals of the Four Masters* (see Mícheál Ó Cléirigh). It was published in seven volumes (1848–51), the original text appearing in a typeface designed by Petrie, with a translation on the facing page. With O'Curry, who in 1854 became professor of archaeology and Irish history in the new Catholic University, O'Donovan opened up new worlds of learning, encouraging the study of Irish history and literature and providing materials to inspire the writers and artists of the Celtic Revival.

O'Donovan's Ordnance Survey work ended in 1842, when the original ambitious programme was curtailed, but he continued to advise on place-names. He studied law at Gray's Inn, London, and was admitted to the Irish Bar in 1847. In 1849, he became professor of Celtic languages at Queen's College, Belfast, but had no students. In 1852, he joined the Brehon Law Commission, formed to publish the *Seanchus Mór* or ancient laws of Ireland, but did not live to complete this monumental work. O'Donovan died of rheumatic fever in Dublin on 9 December 1861.

See A plaque marks O'Donovan's home at 36 Upper Buckingham St, Dublin. He and O'Curry (1794–1862) are buried at Glasnevin cemetery.

(See plate 17)

—49—
SIR SAMUEL FERGUSON
1810–1886
POET AND ANTIQUARIAN

Ferguson was born on 10 March 1810 at 23 High Street, Belfast. Educated at Belfast Academical Institution and Trinity College, Dublin, he studied at Lincoln's Inn, London, before being called to the Irish Bar in 1838. In 1848, he married Mary Guinness, a member of the brewing family, and their home at 20 North Great George's Street, Dublin, became a hospitable focus of intellectual and artistic life. Ferguson practised on the North-East circuit, taking silk in 1859.

As a young man, Ferguson contributed to *Blackwood's Magazine*, and a notable early poem was 'The Forging of the Anchor'. He was a contributor to the influential *Dublin University Magazine* from its beginning in 1833; it published his eerie poem, 'The Fairy Thorn'. In Dublin, he learned Irish and met scholars such as John O'Donovan and George Petrie (*qqv*) and the poet James Clarence

Mangan; he drew extensively on Irish mythology for poems such as 'The Tain Quest' and 'The Death of Dermid'. Works such as *Lays of the Western Gael* (1865) and *Congal* (1872) opened up territory later explored by W. B. Yeats (*qv*), who called Ferguson 'the greatest poet Ireland has produced'. More successful, though, are love songs such as 'The Coolun' and 'The Lark in the Clear Air'.

Ferguson's interest in antiquities may have begun with the great earthwork beside the family home at Donegore, Co Antrim; it was certainly stimulated by Petrie. He wrote many papers for the Royal Irish Academy, of which he became president in 1882. His most important work, *Ogham Inscriptions in Ireland, Wales and Scotland*, was edited for posthumous publication (1887) by his wife. Ferguson gave up his legal practice in 1867, when he was appointed deputy keeper of the public records of Ireland. His thorough reorganisation of the neglected department was recognised with a knighthood in 1878. He died at Howth, Co Dublin, on 9 August 1886.

Politically, Ferguson began life as a unionist, but he later founded the Protestant Repeal Association. He believed there was a plan to 'plebeianise' Ireland by concentrating in London 'all the wealth, refinement and social attractions of the Empire', and sought the restoration of an Irish parliament. Although not a contributor to *The Nation*, his 'Lament for Thomas Davis' (*qv*) is a sympathetic tribute to its co-founder. However, Ferguson was ultimately revolted by the way increasing Irish consciousness led some into violence, and his unease was evident in 'At the Polo-Ground', a poem on the 1882 murder of the chief secretary and under-secretary in Phoenix Park, Dublin.

See A plaque marks Ferguson's Dublin home. He was buried in the churchyard of St John's, Donegore (3 miles/4.5 km ENE of Antrim town).
Read Padraic Colum (ed), *The Poems of Samuel Ferguson* (Allen Figgis, Dublin, 1963).

—50— ISAAC BUTT

1813–1879 FATHER OF HOME RULE

Butt was born in Glenfinn, near Ballybofey, Co Donegal, on 6 September 1813. The only son of a Protestant rector, he was educated at the Royal School, Raphoe, and at Trinity College, Dublin. In 1833, he was a founder of the influential *Dublin University Magazine*, which he edited from 1834 to 1838. He held the chair of political economy from 1836 to 1841. Called to the Irish Bar in 1838, he appeared as a junior for Dublin Corporation when in 1840 it opposed a municipal reform Bill in the House of Lords; although unsuccessful, he was elected an alderman of the reformed Corporation, and proved an effective opponent of the new lord mayor, Daniel O'Connell (*qv*). He took silk in 1844, and was called to the English Bar in 1859.

An opponent of O'Connell's Repeal Association, Butt wrote for Conservative journals in both England and Ireland, and established a Dublin weekly, *The Protestant Guardian*. However, his political conservatism gradually changed; he was deeply moved by the potato famine, and in defending William Smith O'Brien and others involved in the Young Ireland rising of 1848 was critical of misgovernment in Ireland. He became MP for Harwich in 1852, then in that year's general election stood successfully as a Liberal Conservative candidate in Youghal, Co Cork. He held the seat until 1865, but his years in England were marked by growing dissipation and financial difficulty.

Butt returned to Ireland to defend Fenian prisoners, and after a period in a debtors' prison became in 1869 president of the Amnesty Association formed to seek their release. Now a popular national figure, he published in 1870 a pamphlet on 'Irish Federalism', calling for a Dublin parliament with jurisdiction over domestic affairs and continued representation at Westminster. He then formed the Home Government Association, and in 1871 returned to Westminster as MP for Limerick City.

In 1873, he converted the HGA into a more broadly based Home Rule League, and fifty-one Home Rule MPs were returned in the 1874 election. However, Butt was too committed to parliamentary decorum to provide dynamic leadership, and his position was eroded by obstructionists such as Joseph Biggar and Charles Stewart Parnell (*qv*), the latter supplanting him in 1877 as president of the Home Rule Confederation of Great Britain. He died at Dundrum, Co Dublin, on 5 May 1879, and was buried at Stranorlar, Co Donegal.

Read Terence de Vere White, *The Road of Excess* (Browne & Nolan, Dublin, 1946).

—51—
THOMAS DAVIS
1814–1845
YOUNG IRELANDER

Davis was born at Mallow, Co Cork, on 14 October 1814, shortly after the death of his father, an army surgeon. In 1818, his mother and her four children moved to Dublin, settling eventually at 61 (now 67) Lower Baggot Street, where they remained affectionately together until Davis's death. He graduated from Trinity College in 1836, and was called to the Irish Bar a year later; he also spent some time in England and on the Continent, studying languages and building up his library. He published an anonymous pamphlet on *Reform of the Lords* in 1837, joined the National Repeal Association founded by Daniel O'Connell (*qv*), and in 1840 made a notable speech at Trinity's historical society, pleading for studies of Irish history.

Davis's few productive years lay ahead. He began writing for *The Citizen*, a monthly established by leading members of the historical society, and for the Dublin *Morning Register*. Then, in 1841, he and his college friend John Blake Dillon, a barrister, met a young journalist called Charles Gavan Duffy. Duffy shared their burgeoning allegiance to Irish nationhood and independence, and while walking in Phoenix Park they conceived the idea of producing a

George Russell, painted by Hilda Roberts

25 Constance Gore-Booth, later Countess Markievicz, and her sister Eva, in another painting (see plate 22) by Sarah Purser

The entrance to Kilmainham Jail, Dublin

27 J. M. Synge, drawn by John Butler Yeats

28 Seán O'Casey, drawn by Harry Kernoff

29 The Martello tower at Sandycove, Co Dublin, briefly shared by James Joyce and Oliver St John Gogarty, now the Joyce Museum

30 Bust of Michael Collins by Albert Power

31 Death mask of Patrick Kavanagh b Séamus Murphy, and the museum and roun tower at Inniskeen, Co Monaghan

newspaper. Davis was a Protestant, the others were Roman Catholics, and with Duffy as editor they published *The Nation*, whose first weekly issue appeared on 15 October 1842. Its slogan was 'Educate that you may be free'.

Readership soon reached 250,000, outstripping every other Dublin journal and fulfilling its aim 'to direct the popular mind and the sympathies of educated men of all parties to the great end of nationality'. Davis was the principal contributor, and found he could write stirring patriotic ballads such as 'A Nation Once Again' and 'The West's Asleep'. *The Nation* also published John Kells Ingram's 'Who Fears to Speak of '98?', and in 1843 the best songs were reprinted as *The Spirit of the Nation.* Davis also planned a monthly series of shilling volumes forming *The Library of Ireland* (1845–7), in which his own *Literary and Historical Essays* and *Poems* were to influence subsequent patriots.

Although on the committee of the Repeal Association, Davis felt its approach was too sectarian. He and his associates became known as the Young Irelanders, and ultimately they became impatient with O'Connell's rather limited aims, particularly after he accepted a ban on his Clontarf meeting in 1843. Davis and O'Connell quarrelled publicly over the 1845 Colleges Bill, which proposed undenominational university colleges; Davis approved of non-sectarian education, while O'Connell spoke of 'godless education'. What is unknown is whether or not Davis would have supported John Mitchel (*qv*) and other Young Irelanders as they moved towards rebellion in 1848, for he died at home of a fever on 16 September 1845.

See Plaques mark his birthplace at what is now 72 Thomas Davis St, Mallow, and his Dublin home. A statue by John Hogan marks his grave at Mount Jerome cemetery, Dublin. A memorial by Edward Delaney is in College Green, Dublin.
Read M. J. MacManus (ed), *Thomas Davis and Young Ireland* (Stationery Office, Dublin, 1945).

—52—
JOHN MITCHEL
1815–1875
JAIL JOURNALIST

Mitchel was born at Camnish, near Dungiven, Co Londonderry, on 3 November 1815. The son of a Unitarian minister and United Irishman, he was educated in Londonderry and in Newry, Co Down. On leaving Trinity College, Dublin, he entered a solicitor's office in Newry. In 1836, he eloped to England with sixteen-year-old Jane Verner, but was brought back in custody; they eloped again in 1837 and were married. In 1840, he was admitted as a solicitor, practising at Banbridge, Co Down.

In 1842, visiting Dublin, Mitchel met Thomas Davis (*qv*) and Charles Gavan Duffy, and began to write for *The Nation*. When Davis died in 1845, Duffy invited Mitchel to join the newspaper. He subsequently wrote masterly descriptions of districts devastated by the potato famine; he also contributed a life of Hugh O'Neill (*qv*) to *The Library of Ireland* and edited the poems of Davis and James Clarence Mangan. In 1846, Mitchel and other Young Irelanders broke with Daniel O'Connell (*qv*) and his Repeal Association, rejecting the doctrine of 'moral force' and founding the Irish Confederation.

More impatient than Duffy, Mitchel soon left *The Nation*, resigned from the Confederation, and in February 1848 published the first issue of *The United Irishman*. It openly preached sedition to 'that numerous and respectable class of the community, the men of no property', and in May 1848 Mitchel was convicted of treason felony and sentenced to fourteen years' transportation. He hoped his sentence would provoke an insurrection, but nothing more than a skirmish in Co Tipperary ensued.

He was sent to Van Diemen's Land (now Tasmania), where he lived on 'ticket of leave' with his childhood friend John Martin, who had been transported after founding *The Irish Felon* as a successor to Mitchel's defunct publication. In 1853, Mitchel escaped to America, where he published his famous *Jail Journal* (1854). In one entry, Mitchel welcomes the Crimean War, believing an Irish rebellion can succeed only if England is preoccupied elsewhere, and adds 'Give us war in our time, O Lord.' The sentiment influenced Patrick Pearse (*qv*) in 1916.

Mitchel launched several newspapers in America, and as editor of the *Richmond Examiner* championed slavery and the Southern cause; three sons served in the Confederate army, and Mitchel was imprisoned for several months after the Civil War ended. In 1867, he founded the *Irish Citizen* in New York, but angered Fenians by arguing they should give allegiance to their new country. In 1875, he was returned unopposed as MP for Tipperary, but was disqualified as a convicted felon. Returning to Ireland, he was again elected in the subsequent contest, but died at Dromalane, Newry, on 20 March 1875 before he could again be unseated. He was buried in the Unitarian cemetery in High Street, Newry.

—53—
VERE FOSTER
1819–1900
COPY-BOOK PHILANTHROPIST

Foster was born on 26 April 1819 in Copenhagen, where his Anglo-Irish father was British minister. He was a great-grandson of Frederick Hervey (*qv*); his grandmother, Elizabeth Foster (*née* Hervey), became mistress and later wife of the 5th Duke of Devonshire. Educated at Eton and Christ Church, Oxford, Foster also joined the diplomatic service, holding posts in Rio de Janeiro and Montevideo during 1842–7. In 1847, he visited the family estates in Co Louth during the potato famine, and in 1849 toured more distressed counties with his brother Frederick.

Thereafter, Foster committed himself to the welfare of the Irish people. His first thought was to become an enlightened landlord, and he trained for a year at the Glasnevin model farm outside Dublin. He soon concluded that Ireland was overpopulated, and before long had sent forty emigrants to America at his own expense. In 1850, seeking to investigate employment opportunities in the New World, he sailed aboard an emigrant ship and experienced the abuses and cruelties common in such vessels. His letter describing the voyage was published by a parliamentary select committee, and led to remedial legislation.

Returning from America, Foster circulated a 7,000-word broadsheet on emigration, and later published a 'penny emigrant's guide'. In 1852, he established an Irish Female Emigration Fund, proposing that beneficiaries 'of good character' should repay the grants by sending for or assisting relatives in Ireland. Controversy attended his good works, however, when some girls ended up in New York brothels; in Ireland, the loss of cheap labour was sometimes resented, while priests suspected him of proselytism.

Emigration was curtailed by American recession and then by the Civil War, and Foster turned to improving school accommodation and equipment throughout Ireland. Using his own money, he eventually helped to rebuild hundreds of primitive schoolhouses, often facing resistance from the Commissioners of National Education and the Catholic Church. His philanthropy was particularly appreciated by ill-paid teachers, for whom he provided housing, and in 1868 he became first president of the Irish National Teachers' Association.

His other great educational work was to devise copy-books to improve schoolchildren's handwriting and, later, drawing. First issued in 1865, 'Vere Foster Copy Books' were immediately successful throughout the English-speaking world, and helped to finance his other activities. The printing was eventually taken over by a Belfast firm, and in 1867 Foster settled in that city, where he supported many charities. In later life, he renewed his interest in emigration, and in all helped some 25,000 people to leave Ireland. He also edited *The Two Duchesses* (1898), using family correspondence to recount the unusual friendship between his grandmother and Georgiana, Duchess of Devonshire. A bachelor, Foster died in Belfast on 21 December 1900, his fortune reduced to £178.

Read Mary McNeill, *Vere Foster 1819–1900: An Irish Benefactor* (David & Charles, Newton Abbot, 1971).

—54—
DION BOUCICAULT
1820–1890
VAGABOND DRAMATIST

Boucicault was born in Dublin, probably in December 1820. His mother was much younger than her husband, Samuel Boursiquot, a Dublin wine merchant of Huguenot extraction, and her son was presumably fathered by her lover and lodger, Dr Dionysius Lardner. He became the boy's guardian, and paid for his education in Dublin and London. The future dramatist began life as Dionysius Lardner Boursiquot.

In 1828, Lardner took an academic post in London, and Anne Boursiquot took Dion to England, remaining there until she left Lardner in 1836. One of Dion's friends was a playwright's son, and he quickly fell under the theatre's spell, writing a school play called *Napoleon's Old Guard* (1836). He was eventually apprenticed to Lardner to become a civil engineer, but instead set off in 1838 to the English provinces to become an actor. Despite an Irish accent, he had some success under the name Lee Moreton, and his one-act farce *Lodgings to Let* (1839) was performed at the Haymarket theatre in London.

In 1841, his comedy *London Assurance* was a hit at Covent Garden, and for some years he called himself Bourcicault. Success went to his head, however, and he evaded his debts by pleading in court that he was a minor. Boucicault was to steer an erratic course between affluence and bankruptcy throughout his life, but he remained a prolific author and suggested his tombstone might bear the words 'His first holiday'. In 1845, he married Anne Guiot, a moneyed French widow who died soon afterwards, and in 1853, he married the actress Agnes Robertson. Boucicault had many affairs with young actresses, and Agnes finally divorced him in 1889, four years after his bigamous marriage to the young Louise Thorndyke, whom he then married legally.

Boucicault spent much of his time in America, scoring early successes with *The Poor of New York* (1857), with a fire-engine on stage, and *The Octoroon* (1859). However, it was *The Colleen Bawn* (1860), adapted from Gerald Griffin's novel *The Collegians* and depicting a famous Irish murder, that first made him wealthy. The play also helped him to establish authors' entitlement to royalties, instead of the flat payments which were then customary. He and Agnes were also acclaimed in two other Irish melodramas: *Arrah-na-Pogue* (Dublin, 1864) and *The Shaughraun* (New York, 1874), in which he played Conn, the vagabond of the title.

Boucicault had great theatrical flair, and loved spectacular effects such as the railway engine in *After Dark* (1868) and the boat race in *Formosa* (1869). He shrewdly adapted *The Poor of New York* to wherever his companies played, with titles such as *The Poor of Liverpool* and *The Streets of London*. Eventually, though, audiences demanded something more sophisticated than the ageing playwright could provide, and in his last years he taught acting in New York. He died there on 18 September 1890.

Read Richard Fawkes, *Dion Boucicault* (Quartet, 1979).

—55—
JAMES STEPHENS

1824–1901
FIRST FENIAN

Stephens was born in 1824 in Kilkenny, where his father was an auctioneer's clerk. Little is known of his early life, but at twenty he was working on construction of the Limerick and Waterford railway. When the Young Irelanders left the Repeal Association to form the Irish Confederation, Stephens remained aloof from the Confederate clubs. However, he was influenced by the revolutionary ideas of John Mitchel and, as famine gripped Ireland, he and a few intimates drilled secretly.

In July 1848, he joined in the abortive Young Ireland rising, bravely but inadequately led by William Smith O'Brien, which began and ended in a skirmish with police at Ballingarry, Co Tipperary. Wounded in the thigh, Stephens escaped to Paris with Michael Doheny, who later described their adventures in *The*

Felon's Track (1849); in Kilkenny, Stephens' friends pretended he had died, and buried a stone-filled coffin. Stephens spent seven years in Paris, earning a living through teaching and journalism, but also plotting revolution with John O'Mahony, another survivor of Ballingarry.

O'Mahony and Doheny eventually sailed to America, while in 1856 Stephens tramped through Ireland to assess the prospects for a new rising based on a secret conspiracy. On 17 March 1858, Stephens founded the secret Irish Republican Brotherhood in Dublin, and with Thomas Luby Clarke began to gather recruits; a notable capture was Jeremiah O'Donovan Rossa of Skibbereen, Co Cork, and members of his debating club, the Phoenix Society. The IRB's American counterpart became known as the Fenian Brotherhood, and was led by O'Mahony, but Stephens' relations with the Irish Americans were often troubled.

In 1861, the death in San Francisco of another Ballingarry survivor, Terence Bellew McManus, allowed Stephens to stage an impressive funeral at Glasnevin cemetery in Dublin. There was now no doubting Fenianism's strength, and in 1863 he launched a republican newspaper, *The Irish People*. Visiting America in 1864, Stephens promised that 1865 would be 'the year of action', though he knew the movement was badly armed. He chose 20 September 1865, the anniversary of the execution of Robert Emmet (*qv*), for the rising, but the plot was betrayed and his newspaper's offices were raided on 14 September.

Stephens avoided arrest until November, and escaped from Richmond jail within a fortnight, travelling to Paris and then New York. He was now distrusted by the American Fenians and fled to Paris, taking no part in the unsuccessful 1867 rising. He was allowed to return to Ireland in 1891, and lived at Blackrock, Co Dublin. He died on 29 April 1901.

Read Desmond Ryan, *The Fenian Chief: A biography of James Stephens* (Gill, Dublin, 1967); T. W. Moody (ed), *The Fenian Movement* (Mercier Press, Cork, 1968).

—56— P. W. JOYCE

1827–1914
WORDS AND MUSIC

Patrick Weston Joyce was born in Glenosheen, Co Limerick, in 1827. He became a schoolteacher, and eventually principal of Clonmel Model School in Co Tipperary. Model schools were under the control of the commissioners of national education, and were used in the training of teachers; in 1874, Joyce became professor and subsequently principal of the commissioners' training college in Marlborough Street, Dublin. He retired in 1893.

Born in an Irish-speaking area, Joyce was familiar with many native airs. As a young man working in Dublin, he read a prospectus for the Society for the Preservation and Publication of the Melodies of Ireland and called on George Petrie (*qv*). Joyce whistled and hummed many tunes unfamiliar to the older man, and was asked if he would write them down; when he returned within a week with a full notation, it proved the first of many visits. Petrie included thirteen of Joyce's tunes in his 1855 volume, and the Stanford (*qv*) collection of 1902–5 has more tunes from Joyce than from any other collector. As Petrie had succeeded Edward Bunting (*qv*), so he encouraged Joyce to become the third great collector.

In 1873, Joyce published *Ancient Irish Music*, containing 100 unpublished airs from the district of his birth. In 1888, *Irish Music and Song* was the first collection to include verses in Irish; the music was no longer described as 'ancient', an indication perhaps that the antiquarians recognised a living culture. In 1909, Joyce's *Old Irish Folk Music and Songs* contained 842 airs, drawing extensively on the unpublished manuscripts of John Edward Pigot, a Co Cork barrister associated with Thomas Davis (*qv*), and James Goodman, who combined a professorship at Trinity College, Dublin, with a rectorship in Co Cork. When he died in Dublin on 7 January 1914, a manuscript containing some nine hundred more airs was at Joyce's bedside.

Like Petrie, he was a man of parts. He wrote several histories of

Ireland, and collected thirteen Gaelic tales in *Old Celtic Romances* (1879). He wrote a popular study of *English as we Speak it in Ireland* (1910), setting out many dialect variations. Perhaps his best known and most enduring work is *The Origin and History of Irish Names of Places* (three volumes: 1869, 1875 and 1913).

—57— JOHN PENTLAND MAHAFFY

1839–1919 FELLOW OF INFINITE JEST

Mahaffy was born near Vevay, in Switzerland, on 26 February 1839. His father was an Irish clergyman; his evangelical mother had inherited an estate at Newbliss, Co Monaghan, whose rents enabled the young couple to live abroad. In 1848, they returned to look after the Newbliss estate during the potato famine, and had moved to Dublin by the time Mahaffy entered Trinity College in 1855. The outstanding scholar of his year, he graduated with a double first in classics and philosophy in 1859, and was elected fellow and ordained in 1864. In 1865, he married Frances McDougall, a solicitor's daughter.

In 1875, Mahaffy visited Greece for the first time, as paid companion to a Cambridge undergraduate, and was censured by the Trinity College board for making inadequate arrangements during his absence. This did not deter him from a similar visit with Oscar Wilde (*qv*) in 1877. He had already acknowledged Wilde's assistance in his book on *Social life in Greece from Homer to Menander* (1874), which dealt so frankly with homosexuality that he was persuaded to amend later editions. Mahaffy's considerable academic reputation was to rest largely on Greek studies, but he also wrote on Kant and Descartes, and Egyptian studies led to his deciphering papyrus documents discovered by the archaeologist Flinders Petrie. An enemy of provincialism, he opposed the revival of the Irish language as 'a return to the dark ages'.

Mahaffy is best remembered, however, as a character and great all-rounder. He was a talented cricketer, a crack shot, a versatile musician, and a cruelly witty conversationalist whom Oliver St

John Gogarty (*qv*) described as 'the finest talker in Europe'. Typical epigrams attributed to Mahaffy are 'In Ireland the inevitable never happens and the unexpected occurs constantly' and 'An Irish atheist is one who wishes to God he could believe in God.' In 1887, he published *The principles of the art of conversation*, aptly dedicated to 'my silent friends'. A social climber, Mahaffy exploited cricket to gain entry to the vice-regal lodge and other great houses, and went on to enjoy royal acquaintanceships throughout Europe.

He became professor of ancient history in 1871, but it was 1899 before he became one of the seven senior fellows who, with the provost, governed Trinity College. In 1904, he failed to succeed to the provostship, a crown appointment, apparently being judged arrogant and unpopular at a time when imminent university changes required a diplomatic touch. In 1908, he became an energetic first president of the Irish Georgian Society. Provost Anthony Traill died in September 1914; on hearing of his illness, Mahaffy had commented 'Nothing trivial, I hope'. In November, Mahaffy as vice-provost imperiously refused to let 'a man called Pearse' (*qv*) address a Gaelic society meeting inside the college; a few days later, he was appointed provost. In 1917, the government nominated him to the Irish Convention, which sought vainly to solve the Irish question; Mahaffy described himself as a unionist who had 'quietly and silently' drifted towards Home Rule, and proposed an Irish constitution on Swiss lines. He was knighted in 1918, and died on 30 April 1919.

See A plaque marks Mahaffy's home at 38 North Great George's St, Dublin.

Read W. B. Stanford & R. B. McDowell, *Mahaffy: A biography of an Anglo-Irishman* (Routledge & Kegan Paul, 1971).

—58—
JAMES BROWN ARMOUR
1841–1928
'ARMOUR OF BALLYMONEY'

Armour was born at Lisboy, near Ballymoney, Co Antrim, on 20 January 1841. A farmer's son, of Ulster-Scottish Presbyterian stock, he was educated locally and at the Royal Belfast Academical Institution, before entering Queen's College, Belfast, in 1860. His father wanted him to enter the Ministry, but Armour had other ideas and took on part-time tuition to maintain his independence. He then taught in Cookstown, Co Tyrone, for a year before completing his BA at Queen's College, Cork, in 1864; he found the southern city unbigoted and sympathised with Catholic aspirations. Armour hoped to practise law, but his father died in 1864 and a year later he promised a dying brother that he would study for the Ministry. In 1869, he was called to the Second (now Trinity) Presbyterian Church in Ballymoney.

In 1883, Armour married the widowed Jennie Hamilton, a daughter of the manse; her great-grandfather had ministered to the United Irishman William Orr at his execution in 1797, and had been suspected of sedition. A new church was begun in 1884; it was unusual in design, and its octagonal spire (seen by some as evidence of popery) contributed to Armour's defeat in the 1890 election of a professor of church history at Magee College, Londonderry, where he taught part-time from 1885 to 1908.

Armour was an active Liberal; he advocated land reform, and believed the Tories were exploiting Unionism for the benefit of Anglican landlords. In the 1892 general election, Armour supported a Liberal Home Ruler against a Tory Unionist in North Antrim, but he and other Liberals were trounced as Ulster's Protestants declared for the Union.

Armour now faced ostracism and intimidation, but his own congregation remained almost entirely loyal, respecting his unflinching adherence to principle even when they disagreed with him. When he collected over 3,500 Presbyterian signatures commending Gladstone's Home Rule policy, his standing was such that Unionists made every effort to discredit the petition. Armour's nationalism derived essentially from a recognition of injustices; although he favoured secular education, he strongly supported the foundation of the National University (in effect, a successor to Newman's Catholic University) in 1908.

Although warned of a heart condition in 1908, Armour remained an active opponent of Unionism, describing the signing of the 1912 Ulster Covenant as 'Protestant Fools' Day'. In 1913, barracked by an intolerant Presbyterian General Assembly, he posed the question: 'If you deny the right of private judgement and free speech, how much do you have of Protestantism worth preserving? Nothing at all.' He laid much of the blame for the 1916 Easter Rising on the Unionists' gun-running and readiness to resist an Act of Parliament by force, and he argued strongly against Partition. Retiring in 1925, Armour died on 25 January 1928.

Read W. S. Armour, *Armour of Ballymoney* (Duckworth, 1934).

—59—
MICHAEL DAVITT
1846–1906
LAND REFORMER

Davitt was born at Straide, Co Mayo, on 25 March 1846. His father was a Catholic smallholder who in his youth had led an agrarian secret society; evicted after the potato famine, he emigrated with his family to Haslingden, Lancashire, in 1852. Davitt went to work in a cotton mill in 1857, and before long had his right arm amputated after it was caught in a machine. Disabled, he took the opportunity of attending a Wesleyan school.

He joined the Fenian movement in 1865, and in 1867 took part in the abortive attack on Chester Castle. In 1868, he was appointed organising secretary of the Fenians in England and Scotland, becoming a commercial traveller in firearms to conceal his revolutionary activities. In 1870, he was arrested and sentenced to fifteen years' penal servitude for treason felony. He was released from Dartmoor prison on 'ticket of leave' in 1877, largely through the efforts of Isaac Butt (*qv*) and the Amnesty Association.

Davitt joined his family in America, and outlined to Irish American leaders such as John Devoy his plan to link the republican movement with land agitation. Influenced by the economist Henry George, Davitt favoured nationalisation of land, but was prepared to accept peasant proprietorship in place of landlordism. He and Devoy launched the 'New Departure' in alliance with the parliamentary leader, Charles Stewart Parnell (*qv*), who became president of the Irish National Land League founded in 1879.

A broadly based movement, it fought a 'land war' against exorbitant rents and evictions, and in 1881 the government conceded the 'three Fs' of fair rent, fixity of tenure and free sale. Davitt later opposed the 'Kilmainham Treaty' negotiated by Parnell in 1882, but joined him in the Irish National League, successor to the now illegal Land League. He finally rejected Parnell's leadership after the latter's divorce case.

By then, Davitt had served further prison sentences, and in 1886 had married Mary Yore of Michigan; his admirers presented her with a home at Ballybrack, Co Dublin, which became known as 'Land League Cottage'. Davitt was twice elected to parliament and unseated before taking his seat for South Mayo in 1895. He withdrew from Westminster in 1899 as a protest against the Boer War, and died in Dublin on 31 May 1906. For much of his life, Davitt earned a precarious living as a journalist, and his books include *Leaves from a Prison Diary* (1884), *The Boer Fight for Freedom* (1902) and *The Fall of Feudalism in Ireland* (1904).

Visit Davitt memorial museum, opening in 1983, at Straide ($2\frac{1}{4}$ miles/3.5 km NE of Bellavary, Co Mayo). A plaque and high cross mark Davitt's grave, close to a ruined friary.

Read F. Sheehy-Skeffington, *Michael Davitt: Revolutionary Agitator and Labour Leader* (London, 1908; MacGibbon & Kee, 1967); T. W. Moody, *Davitt and Irish Revolution, 1846–82* (Oxford University Press, 1981).

—60—
CHARLES STEWART PARNELL
1846–1891
'THE CHIEF'

Parnell was born at Avondale, Co Wicklow, on 27 June 1846. His father, a wealthy Anglo-Irish landlord, died in 1859; his American mother, Delia, was of Scotch–Irish Presbyterian stock and had inherited an anti-British republicanism from her father, Admiral Charles 'Old Ironsides' Stewart, who had fought in the War of 1812. An arrogant and unruly child, Parnell was largely educated in England; in 1869, he left Magdalene College, Cambridge, after a drunken brawl and took up the life of a country squire. However, the execution of the 'Manchester martyrs' in 1867 had intensified his instinctive hostility to England and in 1875, succumbing to the family tradition of service, he was elected Home Rule MP for Co Meath.

At Westminster, Parnell adopted obstructive tactics so successfully that he became president of the Home Rule Confederation of Great Britain in 1877, president of the Irish National Land League in 1879, and leader of the Irish parliamentary party in 1880. Unlike Isaac Butt (*qv*), Parnell managed to pursue constitutional politics in a manner which won him the approval of Fenians committed to physical force; he shocked the Commons in 1876 by denying that the killing of a constable during the 1867 rescue of Fenian prisoners in Manchester was 'murder'.

Parnell's loose understanding with Michael Davitt (*qv*) and the American Fenian John Devoy was known as the 'New Departure', and stress was laid on the campaign for land reform. Parnell believed that, once reform was achieved, Protestant landlords like himself would have no reason to support the Union with Great Britain. After an unsuccessful attempt to prosecute Parnell for conspiracy, he was arrested in Dublin in October 1881 and held with other Land League leaders in Kilmainham Jail. When they called on their followers not to pay rents, the League was declared illegal. However, there was growing terrorism from secret societies, and Gladstone's government was forced to negotiate the 'Kilmainham Treaty', agreeing to new land reforms in return for an end to agitation. Parnell was released in May 1882, but the assassination of the new chief secretary, Lord Frederick Cavendish, so depressed him that Gladstone had to persuade him to remain in politics.

After the 1885 election, Parnell – variously known as 'The Chief' or 'The uncrowned king of Ireland' – and his eighty-five MPs held the balance of power at Westminster. In 1886, Gladstone committed his government to a Home Rule measure, but it was defeated when ninety-three of his Liberals defected. In 1887, *The Times* published articles entitled 'Parnellism and Crime', but they were shown to be based on forged letters. Parnell's reputation stood high until, in 1889, he was cited as co-respondent in a divorce action brought by an Irish MP, Capt William O'Shea. Katherine O'Shea had been Parnell's mistress since 1880, bearing his three daughters, and the ensuing scandal split the parliamentary party. Parnell later married his 'Queenie', but by then he had been voted out of the party leadership and had lost much of his popular support in Ireland. Worn out by three by-election campaigns, in which Parnellite candidates were defeated, he died in Brighton on 6 October 1891.

Visit Parnell's home at Avondale (1½ miles/2 km S of Rathdrum, Co Wicklow), with three rooms of Parnell memorabilia (open afternoons, May–Sept, Fri–Mon; forest park; guidebook).
See Statue by Augustus St Gaudens in O'Connell St, Dublin, with Parnell's 1885 words: 'No man has a right to fix the boundary to the march of a nation. No man has a right to say to his country: "Thus far shalt thou go and no further". We have never attempted to fix the *ne plus ultra* to the progress of Ireland's nationhood and we never shall.'
Read F. S. L. Lyons, *Charles Stewart Parnell* (Collins, 1977); Paul Bew, *C. S. Parnell* (Gill & Macmillan, Dublin, 1980).

(See plate 18)

—61—
WILLIAM JAMES PIRRIE
VISCOUNT PIRRIE
1847–1924
PIONEER SHIPBUILDER

Pirrie was born of Ulster parents in Quebec, Canada, on 31 May 1847. He spent his childhood at Conlig, Co Down, and was educated at the Royal Belfast Academical Institution before being apprenticed at fifteen to the Harland & Wolff shipyard in Belfast. He worked his way through different departments, becoming head draughtsman, and in 1874 was taken into partnership by the two founders of the firm, Sir Edward Harland and G. W. Wolff. He was to succeed Harland as the shipyard's driving force, and was for many years its chairman.

The introduction of modern steelmaking revolutionised shipbuilding, and Pirrie was at the forefront of developments in marine engineering and naval architecture, particularly in building large ships such as the 46,000-ton *Olympic* (1911) and the 48,000-ton *Britannic* (1914). Harland had formed a connection with the new White Star Line in 1869, and Pirrie's ships maintained their supremacy in the North Atlantic; only illness prevented Pirrie joining the *Titanic* on her ill-fated maiden voyage in 1912. Pirrie's extensive travels helped him to understand and cater for passengers' needs; his 'floating hotels' added substantially to the amenities offered by first class liners. He was also quick to realise the potential of Diesel engines, opening a works near Glasgow for their manufacture.

Both founders of the shipyard had turned to public service, becoming MPs. Pirrie chose instead to serve on Belfast Corporation, becoming lord mayor in 1896–7; he was active in extending the city's boundary, beginning construction of a new City Hall, and launching a scheme to build what became the Royal Victoria Hospital. His initial Unionist views had so weakened that he was refused nomination as a Unionist parliamentary candidate in 1902;

he did not receive an expected knighthood when King Edward VII opened the new hospital in 1903. However, having supported Liberal candidates in the 1906 general election, he soon became Baron Pirrie.

Pirrie's support for the 1912 Home Rule Bill made him unpopular in Belfast, not least among his fellow Protestant industrialists, and he was jeered in the streets after chairing a famous meeting of the Ulster Liberal Association addressed by Winston Churchill. He received his viscountcy in 1921, when King George V opened the new Northern Ireland Parliament, but had no heir. During World War I, Pirrie turned his yards over to warship construction, and inaugurated a large aircraft department. In 1918, he became comptroller-general of merchant shipbuilding, and was energetic in replacing tonnage lost through submarine warfare. He died at sea on 7 June 1924.

—62—

SARAH PURSER

1848–1943
ENTERTAINING ARTIST

Sarah Purser was born in Kingstown (now Dun Laoghaire), Co Dublin, on 22 March 1848. Her father was a prosperous flour miller in Dungarvan, Co Waterford, and she was expensively educated at a Moravian school in Switzerland. Her father's business failure in 1873 saved her from artistic dilettantism. When he emigrated to America, she moved with her mother to Dublin, and studied at the Dublin School of Art and in Paris before launching herself as a portraitist.

After exhibiting at the Royal Hibernian Academy, she was invited to paint the future Countess Markievicz (*qv*) and her sister Eva Gore-Booth. This led to other commissions and, in her own words, she 'went through the British aristocracy like the measles'. Her growing wealth allowed her to foster other artists, and in 1901 she organised a notable exhibition of the paintings of Nathaniel Hone and John B. Yeats. A visitor was Hugh Lane (*qv*), and she painted Douglas Hyde (*qv*) and others for Lane's projected collection of national portraits, begun by Yeats.

Another friend was Edward Martyn (see Lady Gregory), who was advising on a new Roman Catholic cathedral in Loughrea, Co Galway, and wanted to involve Irish artists. The outcome was An Túr Gloine (The Tower of Glass), a workshop for stained glass which Sarah established in 1903 at the rear of 24 Upper Pembroke Street, Dublin. Its most notable artists were to be Michael Healy and Evie Hone.

In 1911, Sarah and her brother John, a professor of medicine, moved into Mespil House (since destroyed), an eighteenth-century mansion beside the Grand Canal. Her monthly salon, 'Miss Purser's second Tuesdays', became an institution for Dublin's artistic and intellectual community and an opportunity for her to exercise a sharpish tongue. A typical comment, on an Irish memoirist, was 'Some men kiss and tell, but George Moore tells and doesn't kiss.'

In 1928, she formed the Friends of the National Collections of Ireland, to purchase pictures and to assist Lady Gregory's campaign for the return of Lane's collection to Dublin. With the establishment of the Irish Free State, Sarah had become friendly with W. T. Cosgrave (*qv*), and in 1928 she persuaded him that Charlemont House in Parnell Square, recently vacated by a government department, should become the Municipal Gallery of Modern Art which Lane had sought. She continued to paint into her eighties, and was almost ninety when she made Oliver St John Gogarty (*qv*) fly her over Mespil House to inspect the roof. She died in Dublin on 7 August 1943.

See St Brendan's Cathedral, Loughrea, is the most representative assembly of works by the artists of An Túr Gloine.
Read Elizabeth Coxhead, *Daughters of Erin: Five Women of the Irish Renascence* (Secker & Warburg, 1965; Colin Smythe, Gerrards Cross, 1979).

(See plates 22 and 25)

—63—
LADY GREGORY

1852–1932
MOVING SPIRIT

Augusta Persse was born on 15 March 1852 at Roxborough House, near Loughrea, Co Galway. She was educated at home, where an early influence was the Anglo-Irish family's Roman Catholic nurse, Mary Sheridan, a fund of Irish folklore and fairy tales. In 1880, she married Sir William Gregory of nearby Coole Park, a retired governor of Ceylon; he was thirty-five years older, and died in 1892.

Lady Gregory edited her late husband's *Autobiography* (1894), and then compiled *Mr Gregory's Letter Box* (1898), dealing with his grandfather's correspondence as Irish under-secretary. Her background reading for the latter book converted her to Home Rule, and she later wrote 'I defy anyone to study Irish history without getting a dislike and distrust of England.' She met W. B. Yeats (*qv*) in London, then at the home of her neighbour, Edward Martyn, and in 1897 they planned a national theatre.

The first production of the Irish Literary Theatre in Dublin was Yeats' *The Countess Cathleen* (1899). In 1904, the Abbey Theatre opened in Dublin with her comedy *Spreading the News* and Yeats' *On Baile's Strand*; a Manchester heiress, Annie Horniman, backed the venture for several years. Lady Gregory wrote over thirty plays, including comedies such as *The Rising of the Moon* (1907) and *The Workhouse Ward* (1908), and 'folk history' plays such as *Kincora* (1905), which drew modern lessons from the story of Brian Boru (*qv*). A director of the Abbey until her death, she was its moving spirit, sustaining it through controversies over plays by Synge, Shaw and O'Casey (*qqv*).

Lady Gregory also met Douglas Hyde (*qv*) at Edward Martyn's house, Tullira. She formed the Kiltartan branch of Hyde's Gaelic League, named from the village at Coole, and wrote often in 'Kiltartan', a stage Irish dialect using grammatical constructions from the native language. She collected folklore enthusiastically and, to encourage interest in Irish mythology, published *Cuchulain of Muirthemne* (1902) and *Gods and Fighting Men* (1904).

Coole Park was the headquarters of the Irish Literary Revival, and attracted many distinguished visitors. Lady Gregory frequently visited London, staying with her nephew Hugh Lane (*qv*); after his death in 1915, she campaigned vigorously for the Lane pictures to be returned from London to Dublin. In later years, she compiled informative reminiscences in *Our Irish Theatre* (1914) and *Seventy Years* (1974) edited by Colin Smythe, and in the *Journals* (1946) edited by Lennox Robinson. During the War of Independence, she contributed articles critical of the Black and Tans to the English weekly, *The Nation*. Roxborough was burnt in the Civil War; Coole was sold to the Irish Land Commission in 1927, but Lady Gregory was able to occupy the house and garden until her death on 22 May 1932.

Visit Coole Park (2 miles/3 km N of Gort, Co Galway); only the outlines of the house remain, but a nature trail (guidebook) includes the garden where the 'autograph tree' bears the initials of famous visitors.

See Memorabilia at Duras House (2¾ miles/4 km NW of Kinvara, Co Galway), a youth hostel, formerly the home of Count Florimond de Basterot, where Lady Gregory and Yeats planned their theatre.

Read Elizabeth Coxhead, *Lady Gregory: A Literary Portrait* (Macmillan, 1961); Colin Smythe, *A Guide to Coole Park, Co Galway* (Colin Smythe, Gerrards Cross, 1973).

(See plate 19)

—64— SIR CHARLES STANFORD

1852–1924
PROLIFIC COMPOSER

Charles Villiers Stanford was born at 2 Herbert Street, Dublin, on 30 September 1852. His father, examiner to the court of chancery, was a keen singer and violoncellist; his mother, daughter of the master in chancery, was a gifted pianist. Their son quickly showed musical talent, composing at eight a march which was performed in the Theatre Royal pantomime, and playing violin, pianoforte and organ. Although Stanford had decided on a musical career, his father insisted on a conventional university education, and he won an organ scholarship at Queen's College, Cambridge, in 1870.

He was immediately active in the university's musical life, and in 1873 was appointed organist of Trinity College, Cambridge. On graduating in classics in 1874, he studied music in Leipzig and Berlin, where he met the young English singer, Jenny Wetton, whom he married in 1878. The early success of his music led to a professorship of composition and orchestral playing at the Royal College of Music, London, in 1883; from 1887, he was also professor of music at Cambridge, and he was much in demand as a conductor. He was knighted in 1902. From 1892, Stanford lived in London, and he died there on 29 March 1924. His ashes were buried in Westminster Abbey.

Stanford was as versatile as he was prolific, and helped to restore the reputation of British composers after a barren period. He wrote operas, of which *Shamus O'Brien* (1896) was the most successful; large-scale choral works such as his 'Requiem' (1897) and 'Stabat Mater' (1907); chamber music; some well-loved church music; solo songs such as 'Songs of the Sea' (1905); and seven symphonies, including the third or 'Irish' Symphony (1887), with its contrasting passages of jig jollity and poignant beauty. Perhaps inevitably, Stanford's reputation waned in later years, particularly in comparison with his contemporary Edward Elgar, and his work was little performed.

Much of the composer's inspiration was drawn from Ireland. He admired the work of Bunting, Petrie and Joyce (*qqv*), and Petrie's daughter entrusted him with her father's manuscripts, from which he published a collection of 1,582 tunes in 1902–5. Stanford's own 'Irish Rhapsodies' drew fruitfully on native melodies, and the stirring fourth rhapsody, 'The Fisherman of Lough Neagh', is a particularly fine example of his orchestral writing. His collected settings of Irish poems for voice and pianoforte include 'An Irish Idyll' (1901), 'Cushendall' (1910), 'A Fire of Turf' (1913) and 'A Sheaf of Songs from Leinster' (1914). Stanford's reflections on his life and times are contained in such books as *Studies and Memories* (1908) and *Pages from an Unwritten Diary* (1914).

See A plaque marks Stanford's birthplace.

—65—
EDWARD CARSON
BARON CARSON OF DUNCAIRN
1854–1935
ULSTER'S ADVOCATE

Carson was born at 4 Harcourt Street, Dublin, on 9 February 1854. His father was an architect of Scottish descent; his mother was descended from one of Cromwell's generals. Educated at Arlington House, Portarlington, Co Laois, and at Trinity College, Dublin, Carson was called to the Irish Bar in 1877, taking silk in 1889. Appointed counsel to the Irish attorney-general in 1887, he earned the nickname 'Coercion Carson' from vigorous prosecutions.

In 1892, Carson was appointed solicitor-general for Ireland, but on being elected Liberal Unionist MP for Dublin University he found himself in opposition. He made his maiden speech at Westminster from the front bench, and quickly established a parliamentary reputation which he enhanced in opposing Gladstone's Home Rule Bill in 1893. In 1894, he became the first Irish QC to take silk in England, and his cross-examination of Oscar

Wilde (*qv*) in 1895 demonstrated his courtroom skills.

In 1900, Carson became solicitor-general in England, and was knighted. In 1905, again in opposition, he resumed his legal practice; in a famous case, in 1910, he established the innocence of a naval cadet, George Archer-Shee, accused of stealing a postal order. (The case was dramatised by Terence Rattigan in his 1946 hit play, *The Winslow Boy.*) In 1910, Carson agreed to lead the Irish Unionist parliamentary party, affirming 'I dedicate myself to your service, whatever may happen.' His loyal lieutenant was Capt James Craig (*qv*), at whose house overlooking Belfast Lough he addressed a large rally in 1911, describing the imminent Home Rule Bill as 'the most nefarious conspiracy that has ever been hatched against a free people'.

On 'Ulster Day', 28 September 1912, a covenant to defeat Home Rule attracted 471,414 signatures. The Ulster Volunteer Force was formed in 1913 and, on the outbreak of World War I, Carson committed its men to the British Army; the Home Rule legislation was suspended. Carson held several wartime posts before resigning in 1918 to fight Ulster's cause again.

Recognising that he could not prevent Home Rule in the rest of Ireland, he opted in 1918 to become MP for the Belfast constituency of Duncairn. When a Northern Ireland parliament was established in 1921, he chose to remain at Westminster, and Craig became the Ulster Unionists' leader and prime minister. Carson became a lord of appeal in 1921, taking a life peerage as Baron Carson of Duncairn. A disappointed man, he concluded that 'I was only a puppet, and so was Ulster, and so was Ireland, in the political game that was to get the Conservative Party into power.' Carson resigned from the bench in 1929, and died at his home in Kent on 22 October 1935. He was buried in St Anne's Cathedral, Belfast.

See Statue by L. S. Merrifield at Parliament Buildings, Stormont, Belfast.

Read H. Montgomery Hyde, *The Life of Sir Edward Carson, Lord Carson of Duncairn* (Heinemann, 1953; Constable, 1974); A. T. Q. Stewart, *Edward Carson* (Gill & Macmillan, Dublin, 1981).

(See plate 20)

—66—
OSCAR WILDE
1854–1900
THE IMPORTANCE OF BEING OSCAR

Oscar Fingal O'Flahertie Wills Wilde was born at 21 Westland Row, Dublin, on 16 October 1854. His father, Sir William Wilde, was an eminent eye and ear specialist and antiquary; his mother, a poetess and folklorist, had contributed to *The Nation* under the pen-name 'Speranza'. The Wildes soon moved to 1 Merrion Square, where Oscar was allowed to frequent his mother's salon.

He was educated at Portora Royal School, Enniskillen, Co Fermanagh, and at Trinity College, Dublin, where he defeated Edward Carson (*qv*) for the foundation scholarship in classics in 1873. At Trinity College he acquired the art of conversation from John Pentland Mahaffy (*qv*), with whom he toured Greece in 1877. In 1874, Wilde won a scholarship to Magdalen College, Oxford, where he was much influenced by John Ruskin, Walter Pater and Cardinal Newman; he became a disciple of aestheticism, pursuing beauty for beauty's sake, and his eccentricity of dress attracted attention. His poem, *Ravenna*, won the Newdigate Prize in 1878.

Wilde's father had died in 1876, his later years clouded by a libel action which his mistress had taken against Lady Wilde. The latter moved to London, as did Oscar, who soon had a reputation for wit. In 1882, he undertook a lecture tour in the United States, advising a customs officer in New York that he had 'nothing to declare but my genius'. In 1884, he married Constance Lloyd, daughter of an Irish barrister, and embarked on a literary career.

His first real success was *The Happy Prince and Other Tales* (1888), but his only novel, *The Picture of Dorian Gray* (1891), offended Victorian susceptibilities. It was the triumph of his play, *Lady Windermere's Fan*, in 1892 that inaugurated his most glorious years, even though the lord chamberlain refused to license a production of *Salomé* because it represented Biblical characters. *A Woman of No Importance* (1893), *An Ideal Husband* (1895) and especially *The Importance of Being Earnest* (February 1895) seemed to ensure a glittering future, as audiences succumbed to such epigrams as 'The truth is rarely pure, and never simple', 'To lose one parent may be regarded as a misfortune . . . to lose both seems like carelessness' and 'All women become like their mothers. That is their tragedy. No man does. That's his.'

However, Wilde had formed a liaison with the young Lord Alfred 'Bosie' Douglas, whose bullying father, the 8th Marquis of Queensberry, publicly accused the playwright of sodomy. In March 1895, Wilde unwisely charged Queensberry with criminal libel, but collapsed under cross-examination by his old rival, Carson. Wilde himself was then charged with homosexual offences, and sentenced in May 1895 to two years' hard labour. A long letter to 'Bosie' was eventually published (1905) as *De Profundis*, and his experiences inspired a poem, *The Ballad of Reading Gaol* (1898).

Wilde last saw his wife in 1896, when she brought news of his mother's death; Constance died in 1898. Wilde was released in May 1897, and immediately left for France; a year later, he toured Italy with 'Bosie'. On 29 November 1900, he was received into the Roman Catholic Church in Paris, and he died a day later from cerebral meningitis.

See Plaques mark Wilde's birthplace and Merrion Sq home.
Read Hesketh Pearson, *The Life of Oscar Wilde* (Methuen, 1946; Macdonald & Jane's, 1975); Vyvyan Holland, *Oscar Wilde and his world* (Thames & Hudson, 1960); H. Montgomery Hyde, *Oscar Wilde* (Eyre Methuen, 1976).

—67—
SIR HORACE PLUNKETT
1854–1932
PIONEER OF CO-OPERATION

Plunkett was born at Sherborne House, Gloucestershire, on 24 October 1854. He was the third son of the 16th Baron Dunsany, whose seat was Dunsany Castle, Co Meath; his mother was a daughter of the 2nd Baron Sherborne. Plunkett was educated at Eton and University College, Oxford, graduating in 1877. In 1879, lung trouble persuaded him to seek a better climate as a rancher in Wyoming. He returned permanently to Ireland in 1889, but visited America annually.

A pioneer of agricultural co-operation, Plunkett established in 1889 the first co-operative creamery in Ireland, at Drumcolliher, Co Limerick. The movement soon spread, and in 1894 he became first president of the new Irish Agricultural Organisation Society, holding office until 1899. In 1891, he had become a member of the Congested Districts Board, and in 1892 he was elected Unionist MP for South Co Dublin. The report of a committee convened on his initiative led to the establishment in 1899 of the Department of Agricultural and Technical Instruction. Plunkett became its political head with the title of vice-president, and held office until 1907, despite losing his seat in 1900. He was knighted in 1903.

Plunkett's slogan, adopted in America by Theodore Roosevelt, was 'Better farming, better business, better living'. He envisaged state aid as an encouragement to self-help, not a substitute for it. In 1907, he was re-elected president of the IAOS, and a year later public subscription purchased a headquarters at 84 Merrion Square, Dublin, known as Plunkett House. However, Plunkett's visionary ideas were largely frustrated by commercial and political interests, and ultimately he enjoyed greater esteem outside Ireland.

While striving to keep his movement non-political, Plunkett himself was converted to Home Rule and in 1914 published an 'Appeal to Ulster not to desert Ireland'. In 1917–18, he chaired the unsuccessful Irish Convention, and in 1919 founded the Irish Dominion League in the hope of keeping Ireland within the British Commonwealth. He became a senator in the new Irish Free State, and republicans responded in 1923 by burning down his house, Kilteragh, Foxrock, Co Dublin.

Soon afterwards, Plunkett settled at Weybridge, in Surrey, where he died on 26 March 1932. During his life, he wrote extensively, including *Ireland in the New Century* (1904) and *The Rural Life Problem of the United States* (1910), and his diaries cover more than fifty years.

Read Margaret Digby, *Horace Plunkett: An Anglo-American Irishman* (Basil Blackwell, Oxford, 1949).

—68— SIR JOHN LAVERY

1856–1941 POPULAR PAINTER

Lavery was born in Belfast in 1856. His father was drowned in 1859, on his way to seek work in America; his mother died of grief, and three orphans were divided among relatives. Lavery went first to an uncle's farm near Moira, Co Down, then at ten to another relative in Saltcoats, Ayrshire. He returned briefly to the farm before finding an apprenticeship to a Glasgow artist and photographer; he studied at the Glasgow School of Art.

At twenty, Lavery set up as an independent artist in Glasgow, enduring poverty until a fire in his studio brought £300 insurance money, which he used to study in London and Paris. In 1886, the Royal Academy accepted his painting of 'A Tennis Party', and it was purchased for a Munich gallery. He became one of the 'Glasgow School' of painters, and was commissioned to paint the state visit of Queen Victoria in 1888; unusually, the Queen agreed to sit for him, and his success as a portraitist was assured. In 1890, he married his Irish model, Kathleen MacDermott, but she died after giving birth to a daughter.

Lavery lived briefly in Rome, then spent five fruitful years in Germany; for many years, he wintered in his house in Tangier. After many rejections by the Royal Academy, he and James McNeill Whistler formed the rival International Society of Sculptors, Painters and Gravers in 1897. In 1910, Lavery married Hazel Trudeau, a widowed American artist little older than his daughter. After acting as a war artist, he was knighted in 1918; he became a British Academician in 1921, and received the freedom of both Belfast and Dublin, to whose municipal galleries he presented many paintings.

Lavery was generally more successful as a painter of women, but an interest in the Irish question led him to paint Griffith, Carson, de Valera, Cosgrave, Collins (*qqv*) and others, drawn carefully from both sides of the politico-religious divide; he also painted the 1916 trial of Roger Casement (*qv*). During the London negotiations on the Anglo-Irish Treaty of 1921, Lavery and his wife entertained extensively at their Cromwell Place home, introducing the Irish delegates to prominent Englishmen; in his autobiography, *The Life of a Painter* (1940), Lavery affirmed 'By many it was believed that had it not been for Hazel there would have been no Treaty – certainly not at the time'.

Lady Lavery had hopes of occupying the vice-regal lodge in Dublin; in the event, she had to be content with having her portrait on the new Irish banknotes, Lavery painting her as the symbolic Cathleen ni Houlihan. She died in 1935. Lavery continued to paint into his eighties – in 1936, he portrayed his encounter with Shirley Temple in Hollywood – and it was perhaps in reaction to long commercial success that his reputation declined after his death at Kilkenny on 10 January 1941.

See The Ulster Museum, Belfast, and the National Gallery and the Hugh Lane Gallery, Dublin, have substantial numbers of Lavery's paintings.

—69—
GEORGE BERNARD SHAW
1856–1950
PROVOCATIVE PLAYWRIGHT

Shaw was born at 3 Upper Synge Street, Dublin, on 26 July 1856. The once prosperous Shaws had come down in the world, and his father was a heavy drinker; his young mother, a fine mezzo-soprano, became attached to a singing teacher, George Vandeleur Lee. In 1871, Shaw became an estate agent's clerk. Soon afterwards, his mother followed Lee to London, and in 1876 Shaw joined her.

A small legacy allowed Shaw to write five novels over the next few years, including *Love Among the Artists* and *Cashel Byron's Profession*, but none got further than magazine serialisation. He was also converted to socialism (and vegetarianism), joining the Fabian Society in 1884. Overcoming his natural shyness, he became an effective public speaker and controversialist. In 1885, a fellow

Fabian persuaded *The Pall Mall Gazette* to employ Shaw as a book reviewer; other opportunities followed, and he was a notable music critic of *The Star* under the pen-name Corno di Bassetto. In 1891, he published *The Quintessence of Ibsenism.*

Shaw's first play was *Widowers' Houses* (1892), and thereafter he wrote prolifically, though not all his plays were immediately performed. *Mrs Warren's Profession*, written in 1893, dealt with prostitution and was banned by the lord chamberlain for more than thirty years. Early plays such as *Arms and the Man*, *Candida*, *Caesar and Cleopatra* and *Captain Brassbound's Conversion* displayed wit and intellectual argument, but Shaw's first real success was the American run of *The Devil's Disciple* (1897). In 1898, he married Charlotte Payne-Townshend, a rich Anglo-Irish Fabian who had nursed him through illness. In 1906, they moved to Ayot St Lawrence, in Hertfordshire.

In 1904, Harley Granville-Barker successfully staged *John Bull's Other Island* at the Royal Court Theatre in London; King Edward VII laughed so much that he broke his seat. In a golden era, the same theatre staged *Man and Superman* (1905), *Major Barbara* (1905) and *The Doctor's Dilemma* (1906). In 1909, Lady Gregory (*qv*) mounted *The Shewing-up of Blanco Posnet* at Dublin's Abbey Theatre after the lord chamberlain had found it blasphemous. *Pygmalion* (1914) was destined to have a second success as the musical comedy, *My Fair Lady*.

Shaw's popularity suffered when in 1914 the *New Statesman* published his manifesto 'Common Sense about the War', suggesting that soldiers of every army might be wise to shoot their officers. Uncompromisingly Irish, he also drew up a petition opposing the execution of Roger Casement (*qv*). However, ex-servicemen enjoyed a revival of *Arms and the Man* in 1919, and he had further success with plays such as *Heartbreak House* (1921) and *Saint Joan* (1923) and political works such as *The Intelligent Woman's Guide to Socialism* (1928). He received the Nobel Prize for Literature in 1925. In old age, Shaw remained a vigorous and provocative personality. When he died at Ayot St Lawrence on 2 November 1950, the National Gallery of Ireland was among the beneficiaries of his will.

See Statue by Paul Troubetzkoy at the National Gallery, Merrion Square, Dublin. A plaque marks Shaw's birthplace, now 33 Synge St, Dublin.
Read Hesketh Pearson, *Bernard Shaw* (Collins, 1942; Macdonald & Jane's, 1975).

(See plate 19)

—70—

E. Œ. SOMERVILLE AND MARTIN ROSS

1858–1949 1862–1915
THE IRISH COUSINS

Edith Œnone Somerville was born on 2 May 1858 in Corfu, Greece, where her father commanded the 3rd Buffs. Her cousin, Violet Martin, was born on 11 June 1862 at Ross House, near Moycullen, Co Galway. Both belonged to that comfortable 'big house' world of the Protestant ascendancy which was increasingly threatened by Catholic nationalism and the Land League; the Martins were one of the original 'tribes of Galway'. They shared a great-grandfather in Charles Kendal Bushe, a former lord chief justice noted for his wit and uncompromising opposition to the Act of Union.

Col Somerville retired to the family home, Drishane, in the village of Castletownshend, Co Cork, in 1859 and the cousins met there in January 1886. It was the beginning of a loving friendship (passionate and obsessive on Edith's part) and literary partnership which was to endure beyond Violet's death. Edith, an accomplished artist, soon began to paint her new companion whom, since she had another cousin Violet, she called by her surname. Martin's elder brother Robert was already a successful London journalist and songwriter ('Ballyhooley' was a music hall hit), and this encouraged the young women to collaborate on illustrated articles; the first, on palmistry, appeared in the London *Graphic* in October 1886. Within a year, they had begun a novel, which was published as *An Irish Cousin* in 1889.

Their most enduring novel, *The Real Charlotte*, appeared in 1894; it is unequalled as a portrait of Anglo-Irish society in the late Victorian era. However, Somerville and Ross (the name taken from the family home) are better known for the three collections of stories which began with *Some Experiences of an Irish R.M.* (1899), and continued with *Further Experiences of an Irish R.M.* (1908) and *In Mr. Knox's Country* (1915). Set in West Cork, they drew particularly on the cousins' knowledge of the hunting field. Edith was master of the West Carberry Hunt for several years and often improved her precarious finances by horse-dealing; it was a hunting accident in 1898 that made Martin a semi-invalid. The adventures of the resident magistrate, Sinclair Yeates, were not universally popular in Ireland for portraying comic peasants and decadent landlords so frankly (if affectionately), but provoked sufficient laughter to elicit testimonials as a cure for quinsy.

The R.M. stories first appeared in magazines, as did many of their travel writings and reminiscences of Irish life which were subsequently collected under such titles as *Some Irish Yesterdays* (1906), *Stray-Aways* (1920) and *Wheel-Tracks* (1923). Edith had a deep interest in spiritualism and, after Martin's death on 21 December 1915, she believed her collaborator continued to communicate through automatic writing at seances. Almost all the later books, including *The Big House of Inver* (1925), a novel inspired by Martin's visit to a ruined house in 1912, and *An Incorruptible Irishman* (1932), a biography of their shared great-grandfather, were published under their joint names. Edith died at Castletownshend on 8 October 1949.

See The cousins are buried beside one another in the churchyard of St Barrahane, Castletownshend, ½ mile/0.8 km from Drishane, which is at the entrance to the village. Ross House, on the edge of Ross Lake, can be seen 3 miles/4.5 km NW of Moycullen, on the Oughterard road.

Read Maurice Collis, *Somerville and Ross: A Biography* (Faber, 1968), drawing on many diaries and letters; Violet Powell, *The Irish Cousins* (Heinemann, 1970).

(See plate 19)

—71— DOUGLAS HYDE

1860–1949 FIRST PRESIDENT

Hyde was born at Castlerea, Co Roscommon, on 17 January 1860. After some years in Co Sligo, his father became rector at Frenchpark, Co Roscommon, in 1866 and Hyde spent his formative years there. He was educated at home, and acquired a knowledge of Irish from native speakers in the district. He had a distinguished and versatile career at Trinity College, Dublin, becoming a doctor of laws in 1888 after he had decided not to take holy orders. In 1890–1, he acted as professor of English literature at the University of New Brunswick, in Canada, teaching also French and German literature.

As a young man, Hyde had published poems in Irish, using a pen-name, An Craoibhín Aoibhinn (the delightful little branch), by which he was later widely known. On his return from Canada, he devoted himself to the preservation of the language; he settled at Ratra House, Frenchpark, and in 1893 married Lucy Kurtz, daughter of a research chemist from Wurtemberg. He had published a collection of folk-tales in Irish in 1889, and many were translated into English in *Beside the Fire* (1890). However, it was *Love Songs of Connacht* (1893), in which his translations accompanied Irish originals, which attracted most attention. The songs had first appeared in the *Weekly Freeman*, conceived as a chapter in a prospective work, *The Songs of Connacht*; other chapters appeared as *Poems ascribed to Raftery* (1903) and *The Religious Songs of Connacht* (1906).

In 1892, Hyde became president of the National Literary Society. Following a presidential address calling for the Irish nation to be 'de-Anglicised', he was invited to chair the 1893 meeting from which emerged the Gaelic League. Hyde was immensely active and successful as its first president, but ultimately he was unable to prevent the League becoming a political battleground. When in 1915 the organisation committed itself to the objective of a 'free,

Gaelic-speaking Ireland', Hyde resigned both the presidency and his membership.

He had become professor of modern Irish at University College, Dublin, in 1909 and he held this post until 1932. However, his best work had been done earlier, and included *The Story of Early Gaelic Literature* (1895) and *A Literary History of Ireland* (1899). He also wrote plays for the Abbey Theatre. Hyde was briefly a senator of the Irish Free State in 1925–6 and again in 1937, but it was as a widely respected figure above politics that in 1938 he was chosen as first president of Ireland under a new constitution. He held office until his term expired in 1945, and died in Dublin on 12 July 1949.

See Hyde is buried in a graveyard 2 miles/3 km WNW of Frenchpark.
Read Dominic Daly, *The Young Douglas Hyde* (Irish University Press, Dublin, 1974).

(See plate 21)

—72— ROGER CASEMENT
1864–1916
THE ROAD TO THE DOCK

Casement was born in Sandycove, Co Dublin, on 1 September 1864. His Protestant father, an army officer who in 1848 had helped Hungarian rebels against Austrian rule, and Catholic mother both died before he was ten, and he was raised by an uncle in Ballycastle, Co Antrim. At twenty, he sailed as a purser to West Africa, and soon joined the explorer Henry Stanley's Congo International Association, whose aims included the suppression of slavery and the improvement of natives' conditions. In 1892, he entered government service, holding consular posts in West and East Africa.

Casement's investigation of the rubber industry in the Congo disclosed a system of slave labour enforced by flogging and mutilation, and his 1904 report led to the eventual abolition of the Congo Free State. However, Casement felt he had enemies within the Foreign Office, and increasingly thought of Ireland as an enslaved and exploited country. He was knighted in 1911, having exposed ill-treatment of Peruvian Indians in rubber plantations, and retired to Ireland in 1913.

Casement immediately became active in the Irish Volunteers. When war broke out in 1914, the Nationalist leader John Redmond encouraged Volunteers to join the British Army; Casement, then visiting America, dissented and sought aid from Germany, which he admired as a colonial power. He had little success in raising an Irish brigade from prisoners of war, but eventually the Germans agreed to send arms in the trawler *Aud* for the planned 1916 rising. Casement, much depressed and sure the rising should be postponed, followed by submarine. Three days before the rising, the *Aud* was captured off the Kerry coast; Casement, who had landed at Tralee Bay, was arrested and taken to London on a treason charge.

The prosecuting attorney-general was F. E. Smith, an outspoken opponent of Home Rule, and in his speech from the dock Casement averred that 'The difference between us was that the Unionist champions chose a path they felt would lead to the Woolsack, [Smith soon became lord chancellor] while I went a road I knew must lead to the dock.' He was sentenced to death, and a campaign for a reprieve lost momentum when copies of the so-called 'Black Diaries' were circulated to demonstrate to influential opinion that Casement had been an active homosexual; controversy has since raged over their authenticity. Stripped of his honours, Casement was hanged on 3 August 1916, having first been received into the Catholic Church. In 1965, his remains were reinterred in Glasnevin cemetery, Dublin.

See A memorial marks Casement's landing at Banna Strand, Co Kerry. Casement monument at Murlough Bay, Co Antrim.
Read René MacColl, *Roger Casement* (Hamish Hamilton, 1956); Brian Inglis, *Roger Casement* (Hodder & Stoughton, 1973).

(See plate 22)

—73—

W. B. YEATS

1865–1939

TOWERING POET

William Butler Yeats was born at 5 Sandymount Avenue, Dublin, on 13 June 1865. He was the eldest child of John Butler Yeats, who moved to London in 1868 to become a painter. Yeats spent many holidays in Sligo with his grandparents, the Pollexfens; in 1880, the family returned to Ireland, and he eventually studied at the Metropolitan School of Art in Dublin. He was influenced by the mysticism of a fellow student, George Russell (*qv*), and developed a lasting interest in theosophy, spiritualism and oriental philosophy. A veteran Fenian, John O'Leary, introduced him to Irish mythology and nationalist literature.

In 1887, back in London, Yeats edited *Poems and Ballads of Young Ireland* for a Dublin publisher. In 1888, he compiled *Fairy and Folk Tales of the Irish Peasantry* for a London publisher, acquiring a reputation as folklorist and poet; in 1889, *The Wanderings of Oisin and other Poems* was well received. He met Maud Gonne (*qv*), but in 1891 and later she rejected his marriage proposals; however, she acted in his patriotic play *Cathleen ni Houlihan* (1902). Under her influence, Yeats became a nominal member of the Irish Republican Brotherhood, and was active in celebrating the centenary of the 1798 rising.

Yeats' first play, *The Countess Cathleen*, launched the Irish Literary Theatre in Dublin in 1899. With Lady Gregory (*qv*), an admirer of his essays in *The Celtic Twilight* (1893), he formed the Irish National Theatre Society in 1902; Yeats' *On Baile's Strand* was performed at the opening of its Abbey Theatre in Dublin in 1904, and he remained a director throughout his life. Among Yeats' plays were *The Land of Heart's Desire* (1904) and *The Words upon the Window Pane* (1930).

More important were his poems, collected in such volumes as *The Wind Among the Reeds* (1899), *In the Seven Woods* (1903), *Responsibilities* (1914), *The Wild Swans at Coole* (1919) and *Michael*

Robartes and the Dancer (1921). Yeats had been politically inactive after Maud Gonne's marriage, and the 1916 rising surprised him. In 'September 1913' he had written 'Romantic Ireland's dead and gone, It's with O'Leary in the grave'. In 'Easter 1916' he wrote 'All changed, changed utterly: A terrible beauty is born'. Later he was to wonder 'Did that play of mine send out Certain men the English shot?' In 1919, he wrote a poem prophetic of Fascism's rise, 'The Second Coming'.

In 1917, Yeats married George Hyde-Lees, an English medium, and they moved to Dublin in 1918; their summer home was Thoor Ballylee, a restored Norman tower in Co Galway. Yeats was an Irish Free State senator for six years, and in a notable speech in 1925 reminded a predominantly Roman Catholic assembly that the Protestant minority were 'no petty people. We are one of the great stocks of Europe. We are the people of Burke; we are the people of Grattan; we are the people of Swift, the people of Emmet, the people of Parnell.' Among many honours, he received the Nobel Prize for Literature in 1923. In 1932, he and George Bernard Shaw (*qv*) founded the Irish Academy of Letters.

Among his later volumes, *The Tower* (1928) and *The Winding Stair and Other Poems* (1933) confirmed Yeats' place among the greatest poets of the English language. Declining health forced him to spend winters abroad, and he died at Cap Martin, on the French Riviera, on 28 January 1939. In 1948, his remains were reinterred at Drumcliffe, Co Sligo, in the shadow of Ben Bulben, a region which inspired 'The Lake Isle of Innisfree' and many other poems.

Visit The regions around Sligo and Gort, Co Galway, have many associations with Yeats. Particularly rewarding is Thoor Ballylee (4 miles/6 km NE of Gort, signposted from the Galway and Loughrea roads), now a Yeats museum (open daily, Mar–Oct; guidebook). There is also a Yeats Memorial Museum with the Sligo County Library and Museum, Stephen St, Sligo.

See A plaque marks Yeats' home at 82 Merrion Sq, Dublin.

Read Joseph Hone, *W. B. Yeats, 1865–1939* (Macmillan, 1942); Sheelah Kirby, *The Yeats Country* (Dolmen Press, Dublin, 1962); Micheál Mac Liammóir and Eavan Boland, *W. B. Yeats and his world* (Thames & Hudson, 1971).

(See plates 19 and 23)

—74—

MAUD GONNE MacBRIDE

1865–1953
IRELAND'S JOAN OF ARC

Maud Gonne was born near Aldershot, in England, probably on 20 December 1865. Her father was a captain in the 17th Lancers; after her mother died of tuberculosis in 1871, Maud and her younger sister were largely educated by a governess on the French Riviera. Her father, now a colonel, was posted to Dublin Castle in 1882. Maud, already a beauty, acted as his hostess, but Col Gonne died of typhoid fever in 1886.

The girls lived briefly with an uncle in London, but Maud contracted a lung haemorrhage and was sent to recover at Royat, in the French Auvergne. There she met Lucien Millevoye, a journalist and politician, whose marriage had broken down. They agreed to work together for Irish independence and for French recovery of Alsace-Lorraine from Germany. Maud had been much affected by the sight of evictions in Ireland and, although she was English, did not discourage Millevoye's suggestion that she become Ireland's Joan of Arc. She was to bear him two children, one dying in infancy, before their affair ended in 1898.

For several years, she divided her life between Ireland, London and France. Through the Fenian John O'Leary she met W. B. Yeats (*qv*), with whom she founded an Association Irlandaise in Paris; in 1891, she rejected his marriage proposal. She belonged for a period to the secret Irish Republican Brotherhood, and her protests against evictions and against celebration of Queen Victoria's diamond jubilee attracted police attention.

In 1900, she founded Inghinidhe na hÉireann (Daughters of Ireland), a women's republican movement, and opposed British recruitment for the Boer War. In 1902, she took the title role in Yeats' *Cathleen ni Houlihan*, symbolising Ireland's struggle when she shed the appearance of an old crone to become 'a young girl with the walk of a queen'. In 1903, she married in Paris Maj John MacBride, who had formed an Irish brigade to fight on the Boers' side; he was a Roman Catholic, and she had lately become one. Their marriage was a failure within two years, and he returned to Ireland, where he was executed after the 1916 rising. She spent most of her time in France.

Returning to Dublin in 1917, she was interned in 1918, spending several months in Holloway prison in London. Later she worked with the White Cross movement, organising relief during the War of Independence. During the Civil War, she formed the Women's Prisoners' Defence League to assist republican prisoners and their dependants. Imprisoned in 1923, she was soon released when she went on hunger strike. In 1938, she published *A Servant of the Queen*, an account of her early life. From 1922, Madame MacBride (as she was known) lived at Roebuck House, Clonskeagh, Dublin, where she died on 27 April 1953. She was buried in Glasnevin cemetery.

Read Samuel Levenson, *Maud Gonne* (Cassell, 1976); Elizabeth Coxhead, *Daughters of Erin: Five Women of the Irish Renascence* (Secker & Warburg, 1965; Colin Smythe, Gerrards Cross, 1979).

—75—
GEORGE RUSSELL
1867–1935
'AE'

Russell was born in Lurgan, Co Armagh, on 10 April 1867. His father, a book-keeper, moved in 1878 to Dublin, where Russell eventually attended the Metropolitan School of Art. A fellow student was W. B. Yeats (*qv*), who introduced him to theosophy. As a boy, Russell had had mystical experiences, and theosophy provided an intellectual framework for his insights into the nature of God and the universe. His eventual pen-name 'AE' was a compositor's misreading of 'Æon', the name given by Gnostics to the earliest beings separated from God.

In 1890, Russell became a draper's clerk, but lived in a community of theosophists at 3 Ely Place; another member was Violet North, an Englishwoman with psychic powers. In 1894, he published his first book of verse, *Homeward: Songs by the Way*. He also became interested in Irish history and mythology, finding parallels with his reading in Eastern philosophy. *The Earth Breath and other Poems* (1897) drew on Celtic legend. In 1897, on Yeats' recommendation, he was employed by Horace Plunkett (*qv*) in the Irish Agricultural Organisation Society.

In 1898, Russell became assistant secretary of the IAOS. He married Violet North, and their home became one of Dublin's intellectual meeting places. Russell was editor of the IAOS weekly, *The Irish Homestead*, from 1905 to 1923, when it amalgamated with *The Irish Statesman*, which he edited until it closed in 1930. *The Irish Homestead* was a remarkable journal, whose philosophical observations on rural civilisation appealed to English and American thinkers as much as to Ireland's farmers.

In 1917, Russell warned in a pamphlet against the partition of Ireland, arguing that it would destroy the balance between industrial North and agricultural South and perpetuate hatred. He was nominated to the 1917 Irish Convention, proposing Plunkett as chairman, but resigned in 1918 in the correct belief that the Convention would not solve the Irish problem. During the Civil War, he published an open letter appealing to republicans to raise the conflict 'from the physical to the intellectual plane'.

Editing *The Irish Statesman*, Russell became involved in the major controversies of the new state. Violet Russell died in 1932 and, when Eamon de Valera (*qv*) formed a government, Russell felt that the achievements of the Irish Free State would be endangered in a Gaelic, Church-dominated society. In 1933, he moved to England, and he died in Bournemouth on 17 July 1935. He was buried in Mount Jerome cemetery in Dublin.

See A plaque marks Russell's home at 17 Rathgar Ave, Dublin.
Read Henry Summerfield, *That Myriad-Minded Man: a biography of George William Russell, "A.E.", 1867–1935* (Colin Smythe, Gerrards Cross, 1975).

(See plates 19 and 24)

—76— EOIN MacNEILL

1867–1945 LEADING SCHOLAR

John MacNeill, as he was baptised, was born in Glenarm, Co Antrim, on 15 May 1867. Son of an ex-seaman, he was educated at St Malachy's College, Belfast, and continued studying there for a degree in the Royal University. In 1887, he won a clerkship in the Four Courts in Dublin, and while working there completed his BA. He began to study Irish, and in 1891 visited the Aran Islands to learn the spoken language. In 1893, an article by him in the *Gaelic Journal*, on the preservation of Irish, led to the foundation of the Gaelic League; he became honorary secretary and Douglas Hyde (*qv*) president.

Although the League suffered conflicts of policy and personality, over four hundred branches were formed within ten years. MacNeill became editor of the monthly *Gaelic Journal* in 1894, and of the new weekly *An Claidheam Soluis* (The Sword of Light) in 1899, then vice-president of the League in 1903. He became a member of the senate of the new National University of Ireland in 1908, and a year later left the Four Courts to become professor of early Irish history at University College, Dublin. He argued strongly and successfully that Irish should be a compulsory matriculation subject in the new university; from his historical writings, such as *Phases of Irish History* (1919) and *Celtic Ireland* (1921), it is evident that MacNeill saw the language as an essential element in Irish nationality.

In November 1913, he contributed an influential leading article, 'The North Began', to *An Claidheam Soluis*, calling for the formation of Irish Volunteers in response to the Unionists' Ulster Volunteer Force. He became president and later chief of staff of the Volunteers, seeing them as a means of ensuring that Home Rule would be implemented. However, when in 1916 he discovered that Patrick Pearse (*qv*) and others planned to turn Volunteer manoeuvres into an armed rising, he cancelled orders for Easter Sunday parades. None the less, the abortive rising began on Easter Monday, and a court-martial later sentenced MacNeill to penal servitude for life. While in Dartmoor prison, in England, he was elected president of the Gaelic League.

MacNeill was released in 1917 under an amnesty, and in 1918 was elected Sinn Féin MP for both Londonderry and the National University. He became minister of finance and then of industries in the First Dáil, and, after six months' imprisonment in 1920–1, speaker of the Second Dáil. Accepting the 1921 Anglo-Irish Treaty, he became minister of education in the first Irish Free State administration. In 1923, he was also appointed to the Boundary Commission set up to determine the border between the two parts of a partitioned Ireland, but resigned in 1925 after a largely accurate newspaper forecast that only minor changes in the existing border would be recommended. He also left the government, and after 1927 devoted himself to scholarship, becoming in 1928 first chairman of the Irish Manuscripts Commission. He died in Dublin on 15 October 1945.

Read F. X. Martin & F. J. Byrne (eds), *The Scholar Revolutionary: Eoin MacNeill, 1867–1945, and the Making of the New Ireland* (Irish University Press, Shannon, 1973); Michael Tierney, *Eoin MacNeill: Scholar and Man of Action, 1867–1945* (Clarendon Press, Oxford, 1980).

—77—
CONSTANCE MARKIEVICZ
1868–1927
REBEL COUNTESS

Constance Gore-Booth was born in London on 4 February 1868. She was the eldest child of Henry Gore-Booth, soon to become 5th baronet and inherit estates at Lissadell, Co Sligo. Constance and her sister Eva were recalled in a poem by W. B. Yeats (*qv*), who wrote 'The light of evening, Lissadell, Great windows open to the south, Two girls in silk kimonos, both Beautiful, one a gazelle'. She had an adventurous nature, and was a noted horsewoman.

In 1893, Constance enrolled at the Slade School in London, and in 1898, she continued her art studies in Paris, where she met Count Casimir Dunin-Markievicz. He was Polish, six years younger, a painter and Roman Catholic; his estranged wife was dying in the Ukraine. Constance and Cassie were married in London in 1900, and eventually settled in Dublin in 1903. Their life embraced Dublin Castle society, the Abbey Theatre and the Gaelic League.

In 1906, they rented a cottage at Balally, in the Dublin mountains. The poet Padraic Colum had lived there, and had left old copies of *Sinn Féin*; reading them, Constance was converted to the cause of Irish independence. In 1908, she joined Inghinidhe na hÉireann (Daughters of Ireland), founded by Maud Gonne MacBride (*qv*), and took part in a Sinn Féin demonstration, effectively severing her links with Dublin Castle. In 1909, she founded Na Fianna Éireann, a republican movement for boys, who received arms training at the cottage.

Attracted to the socialism of James Connolly and James Larkin (*qqv*), Countess Markievicz organised a soup kitchen during the 1913 strike in Dublin. Her neglected husband soon returned to the Ukraine, and was not seen in Dublin again until 1924. She joined the Irish Citizen Army, and in the 1916 rising occupied the College of Surgeons at St Stephen's Green. Her death sentence was commuted; while in Aylesbury prison, in England, she was elected president of Cumann na mBan, the women's auxiliary force of the Irish Volunteers.

Released in 1917, she was immediately received into the Catholic Church. Arrested again in 1918, she was in Holloway prison when elected Sinn Féin MP for a Dublin constituency; the first woman elected to Westminster, she sat instead on her release in the separatist Dáil Éireann, becoming minister for labour. She served further sentences in Irish jails, was released under the 1921 truce, and rejected the subsequent Anglo-Irish Treaty. She toured America in the republican cause and, during the Civil War, edited a republican weekly in Glasgow. Countess Markievicz eventually joined the Fianna Fáil party formed by Eamon de Valera (*qv*), and was elected to the Dáil shortly before her death in Dublin on 15 July 1927. She was buried in Glasnevin cemetery.

Visit Lissadell House (8 miles/13 km N of Sligo) (open afternoons, May–Sept, Mon–Sat).

See Bust by Séamus Murphy in St Stephen's Green, Dublin. **Read** Seán O'Faoláin, *Constance Markievicz* (Cape, 1934; Sphere Books, 1967); Anne Marreco, *The Rebel Countess: The Life and Times of Constance Markievicz* (Weidenfeld & Nicolson, 1967).

(See plate 25)

—78—
JAMES CONNOLLY
1868–1916
REVOLUTIONARY SOCIALIST

Connolly was born in Cowgate, Edinburgh, on 5 June 1868. His Irish Catholic parents were poor, and Connolly worked from the age of eleven; in 1882, he falsified his age to join the army. Stationed in Dublin in 1889, he deserted to avoid foreign service, and in 1890 married Lillie Reynolds, a Protestant domestic servant from Co Wicklow. They settled eventually in Edinburgh.

Connolly was active in the Scottish Socialist Federation and the Independent Labour Party, but lost his job and became paid organiser of the Dublin Socialist Club in 1896. Soon he had founded and become secretary of the Irish Socialist Republican Party. In 1898, he launched the weekly *Workers' Republic*, exploiting the 1798 centenary to argue that the principles of Wolfe Tone (*qv*) could only be realised in a socialist republic.

When Connolly returned from a 1902–3 American tour, he found the ISRP in disarray, and became paid organiser of the new Socialist Labour Party in Scotland. Unable to make a living, he emigrated to America, where he helped to found the International Workers of the World (the 'Wobblies') in 1905. In 1907, he founded the Irish Socialist Federation in New York, expounding his Marxist views in its monthly journal, *The Harp*.

Connolly returned to Ireland in 1910, joining the Socialist Party of Ireland, successor to the ISRP. He soon published *Labour, Nationality and Religion*, defending a Catholic's right to be a socialist, and *Labour in Irish History*, describing the working class as 'the incorruptible inheritors of the fight for freedom in Ireland'.

In 1911, he became Ulster organiser of the Irish Transport and General Workers' Union, which James Larkin (*qv*) had founded in 1909, and soon called a dock strike in Belfast. When Larkin was imprisoned in 1913, Connolly forced his release by closing the port of Dublin.

Larkin left for America in 1914, and Connolly became acting general secretary of the ITGWU, commandant of the recently formed Irish Citizen Army, and editor of the *Irish Worker*, soon suppressed for its anti-war sentiments. He was persuaded by the Irish Republican Brotherhood to support the 1916 rising, and about 120 ICA members took part on Easter Monday. Connolly was commandant-general in Dublin, and led the assault on the General Post Office. His left ankle was smashed by a bullet during the subsequent week's fighting, and after his court-martial he was strapped to a chair and shot at Kilmainham Jail on 12 May 1916.

Visit Kilmainham Jail museum, Dublin (open Sun afternoons).
Read Samuel Levenson, *James Connolly* (Martin Brian & O'Keeffe, 1973); Ruth Dudley Edwards, *James Connolly* (Gill & Macmillan, Dublin, 1981).

—79—

ERSKINE CHILDERS

1870–1922
'DAMNED ENGLISHMAN'

Childers was born in London on 25 June 1870. His English father, an Oriental scholar, died of tuberculosis in 1876; his Anglo-Irish mother (*née* Barton) died of the same disease in 1884. Much of Childers' childhood was spent at his mother's home, Glendalough House, Annamoe, Co Wicklow; at nineteen, sciatica gave him a permanent limp.

He was educated in England, and in 1895 became a committee clerk in the House of Commons. When the Boer War broke out in 1899, he quickly joined the City Imperial Volunteer battery of the Honourable Artillery Company, and his war diary was published as *In the Ranks of the C.I.V.* (1900). He wrote two war histories, and campaigned against the use of antiquated cavalry. However, Childers' reputation as an author rests on *The Riddle of the Sands* (1903), a novel drawing on his yachting experiences exploring the Friesian coast; his story of two yachtsmen chancing on a German plan to invade England impressed readers fearful of German militarism.

In 1903, he married Molly Osgood, daughter of a Boston doctor and afflicted with a greater limp; Dr Osgood's wedding present was a yacht, the *Asgard*. Although the Boer War had made him question Britain's imperial role, Childers did not espouse Home Rule until 1908, when he inspected Irish agricultural co-operatives with his cousin, Robert Barton, and warmed to the ideas of Sir Horace Plunkett (*qv*). He resigned from the Commons in 1910, and in 1911 advocated dominion status in *The Framework of Home Rule*.

Following the Ulster gun-running of April 1914, Childers undertook a similar exploit in the *Asgard*, landing arms for the Irish Volunteers at Howth, Co Dublin, on 26 July 1914. None the less, he served in both the Royal Navy and the Royal Air Force in World War I, believing the Allies were committed to the independence of small nations. In 1917, he was seconded to the secretariat of the Irish Convention, which failed to agree on implementing Home Rule.

Demobilised in 1919, he accompanied Arthur Griffith (*qv*) on an unsuccessful delegation to the Versailles peace conference. He settled in Dublin, becoming publicity director for Dáil Éireann, to which he was elected in May 1921. After the July truce, he accompanied Eamon de Valera (*qv*) to London for negotiations, then became secretary to the Irish delegation which negotiated the Anglo-Irish Treaty.

By now a fanatical republican, Childers favoured de Valera's 'external association' formula, and bitterly opposed the treaty in the Dáil. Griffith responded with 'I will not reply to any damned Englishman in this assembly', and later accused Childers of being an English agent. During the Civil War, Childers produced republican propaganda, but the former British officer became increasingly isolated among the guerillas of Co Cork. On 10 November 1922, he was captured at Glendalough House, and after a court-martial was executed in Dublin on 24 November 1922. In 1973, his son and namesake became fourth president of Ireland.

Visit The Kilmainham Jail museum, Dublin, features material on the gun-running; the *Asgard* is on display (open Sun afternoons). **Read** Andrew Boyle, *The Riddle of Erskine Childers* (Hutchinson, 1977).

—80—
JAMES CRAIG
1st VISCOUNT CRAIGAVON
1871–1940
UNIONISM'S ROCK

Craig was born at Sydenham, Belfast, on 8 January 1871. His father was a Presbyterian whiskey distiller, a self-made millionaire who soon bought a substantial house, Craigavon, overlooking Belfast Lough. Educated at Merchiston Castle, Edinburgh, Craig became a successful stockbroker and a founder member of the Belfast Stock Exchange. Following the outbreak of the Boer War, he was commissioned in the Royal Irish Rifles and served with the Imperial Yeomanry. When captured by the Boers in 1900, he chose to march 200 miles with his men rather than ride with the officers; released because of a war wound, he became a railway staff officer before being invalided home with dysentery.

A legacy enabled him to turn to politics, and he won East Down as a Unionist in 1906; he remained at Westminster until 1921, latterly representing Mid-Down. In 1911, when a new Home Rule Bill was imminent, Craig staged a massive unionist demonstration at Craigavon, at which Sir Edward Carson (*qv*) assumed the leadership of northern Protestants. Craig's organisational skills and cool courage were the rock on which Carson's oratory built Ulster unionism into a powerful force.

With the outbreak of war in 1914, Home Rule was put into abeyance. Craig immediately offered the Ulster Volunteer Force, which had been drilling since 1912, to the British Army. It became the 36th (Ulster) Division, suffering heavy casualties at the Somme in 1916; ill health denied Craig active service, and he had resigned his commission earlier in the year. He subsequently held minor government posts, and became a baronet in 1917.

In 1920, a new parliament was established for six of the nine Ulster counties. With Carson opting to remain at Westminster, Craig became Northern Ireland's first prime minister, and in 1922 the Unionist majority voted to remain within the United Kingdom. In violent times, Craig had to establish a new police force, the Royal Ulster Constabulary, supported by a special constabulary and equipped with exceptional powers; however, while restoring order, he also attempted to reach some understanding with southern leaders such as Eamon de Valera and Michael Collins (*qqv*), and was more tolerant of the Catholic minority in Northern Ireland than most of his supporters.

Craig proved less effective at the more mundane tasks of government, and for the rest of his life he headed an ageing cabinet which made little progress on the province's social and economic problems. However, he remained resolute in defence of Northern Ireland's constitutional position, and ensured that the boundary commission set up under the 1921 Anglo-Irish Treaty did not reduce its territory. In 1927, he became Viscount Craigavon of Stormont. He died at Glencraig, Co Down, on 24 November 1940, and was buried in the grounds of the Northern Ireland parliament.

Read Patrick Buckland, *James Craig, Lord Craigavon* (Gill & Macmillan, Dublin, 1980).

—81—
A. M. SULLIVAN
1871–1959
THE LAST SERJEANT

Sullivan was born in Drumcondra, Dublin, on 14 January 1871. He was named after his father, Alexander Martin Sullivan, editor and proprietor of *The Nation*, who had served three months in prison for an article on the execution of the 'Manchester martyrs' in 1867; he used the money from a subsequent testimonial to erect a statue of Henry Grattan (*qv*) in College Green, Dublin, and became a Westminster MP from 1874 to 1881. His son also practised journalism on leaving Trinity College, Dublin, was called to the Irish Bar in 1892, and took silk in 1908.

Sullivan's skill as an advocate brought early advancement. He became third king's serjeant in 1912, second serjeant in 1918, and first serjeant in 1920. The office was an ancient one, its occupants wearing in their wigs a small piece of black cloth known as a coif. When it was abolished with the establishment of the Irish Free State, Sullivan retained the courtesy title; its English counterpart had disappeared in Victorian times.

Throughout his life, Sullivan was committed to constitutional politics. He opposed equally the 'physical force' republicans and the Black and Tans, and in a lawless period courageously upheld the administration of justice through the established courts. In January 1920, he survived an attempt on his life near Tralee, Co Kerry; later, shots were fired at a railway carriage in which he was travelling.

Sullivan had been admitted to the English Bar in 1899, and in 1916 he was persuaded to undertake the defence of Roger Casement (*qv*); Casement's solicitor was George Gavan Duffy, Sullivan's brother-in-law and son of Charles Gavan Duffy, co-founder of *The Nation*. Sullivan had never practised in England, where he ranked only as a junior counsel, and he broke down from nervous exhaustion during his concluding speech.

Despite this failure, he took silk in England in 1919, and moved there after the establishment of the Irish Free State in 1922. As Serjeant Sullivan, he became a popular figure, and was elected treasurer of the Middle Temple in 1944; occasionally reckless in court, he combined a grave presence with an ironic wit cultivated in a country where, as he put it, 'The administration of justice was not hindered by the passing jest.' Among his most notable cases was the libel action brought by the birth control pioneer, Marie Stopes, against Dr Halliday Sutherland, whom Sullivan successfully defended.

He published two books of reminiscence, *Old Ireland* (1927) and *The Last Serjeant* (1952), giving a vivid portrait of courts in both countries. When Ireland became a republic in 1949, Sullivan felt he was now an alien disqualified from practising in England. He returned to Dublin, but retained a house at Beckenham, Kent, where he died on 9 January 1959.

—82—

ARTHUR GRIFFITH

1871–1922
ARCHITECT OF SEPARATISM

Griffith was born at 4 Dominick Street, Dublin, on 31 March 1871. His father was a printer, and Griffith himself was apprenticed as a compositor. In 1897, he sailed to South Africa, partly for health reasons, and edited an English weekly newspaper in the Transvaal. Griffith's sympathies were with the Boers, and the paper soon closed; he later worked in goldmining, and organised a parade in Johannesburg to celebrate the centenary of the 1798 rising.

Returning to Dublin, he and William Rooney founded a weekly newspaper, *The United Irishman*, named after one associated with John Mitchel (*qv*) in 1848. Griffith wanted members of the Irish parliamentary party to stay away from Westminster. His articles were republished as *The Resurrection of Hungary*, *A Parallel for Ireland* (1904), drawing the lesson that Hungarians had won independence from Austria in 1867 by refusing to send representatives to the parliament in Vienna.

In 1903, Griffith formed the National Council, and at its annual convention in 1905 elaborated his ideas under the name Sinn Féin (Ourselves). Griffith was prepared to retain the crown in a dual monarchy system, but he looked back to 1783 and Westminster's brief renunciation of the right to legislate for Ireland. When *The United Irishman* was bankrupted by a libel action in 1906, Griffith launched a new publication, *Sinn Féin*. A Sinn Féin party gradually emerged, and Griffith became president in 1911; he joined the Irish Volunteers in 1913. An opponent of insurrection, Griffith took no part in the 1916 rising, but was later interned in England until the end of the year; it was widely but inaccurately described as a Sinn Féin rising, and Griffith's party gained new impetus.

He yielded the presidency to Eamon de Valera (*qv*) in 1917, and Sinn Féin's successes in the 1918 election paved the way to the War of Independence. Dáil Éireann, the alternative assembly which Griffith had envisaged, met in January 1919, and he became minister for home affairs and deputy president. Griffith led the delegation which negotiated the 1921 Anglo-Irish Treaty. After the Dáil had rejected de Valera's opposition to its terms, Griffith was elected president of the Dáil and of the 'Republic of Ireland' which was soon to be replaced by the Irish Free State. The treaty was further endorsed in the general election of June 1922, but the Civil War broke out soon afterwards. Griffith, exhausted by his labours, died suddenly in Dublin on 12 August 1922, and was buried in Glasnevin cemetery.

See Memorial at Leinster Lawn, Merrion Sq, Dublin.
Read Padraic Colum, *Arthur Griffith* (Browne & Nolan, Dublin, 1959); Calton Younger, *Arthur Griffith* (Gill & Macmillan, Dublin, 1981).

—83—

J. M. SYNGE

1871–1909
MAN OF ARAN

John Millington Synge was born at 2 Newtown Villas, Rathfarnham, Dublin, on 16 April 1871. His father was a land-owning barrister who died in 1872; his mother was the daughter of an evangelical rector from Co Antrim. Synge himself read Charles Darwin at fourteen, and gradually renounced Christianity. An asthmatic child, he was educated privately before entering Trinity College, Dublin, where he graduated in 1892. An accomplished violinist, Synge studied music in Dublin and in Germany, but abandoned a musical career in 1894 and moved to Paris to teach English and study at the Sorbonne.

In 1896, he met W. B. Yeats (*qv*), who advised him to visit the Aran Islands and 'express a life that has never found expression'. Returning to Ireland in 1897, he was operated on for a growth in his neck, a first sign of Hodgkin's disease. In May 1898, he reached the Aran Islands; during the next six weeks, he took photographs and filled his notebooks, learning Irish and listening to the stories which provided raw material for almost every play he wrote. Through

Yeats, Synge was invited to stay with Lady Gregory (*qv*), and took part in discussions on the proposed Irish Literary Theatre. He continued to live in Paris, contributing to several literary journals, but made annual visits to Aran.

Synge's one-act play, *The Shadow of the Glen*, was performed in Dublin in 1903; its portrait of a loveless rural marriage caused some offence. *Riders to the Sea* followed in 1904, and both plays were quickly staged in London. In 1905, *The Well of the Saints* was ill received at the Abbey Theatre. Synge's friend, the poet John Masefield, had earlier commissioned two articles for the *Manchester Guardian*, and the newspaper subsequently asked Synge to write a series on the 'congested districts' of Connemara and Co Mayo, with illustrations by Jack B. Yeats (*qv*).

Synge had fallen in love with a young Catholic actress, Molly Allgood, sister of the Abbey star Sara Allgood. Under her stage name of Maire O'Neill, she played Pegeen Mike when *The Playboy of the Western World* opened at the Abbey in 1907. His finest work, it was greeted with rioting; audiences were initially unwilling to accept its unflattering comic portrayal of peasant life, and were puritanically shocked by a reference to 'females standing in their shifts'. Arthur Griffith and Patrick Pearse (*qqv*) were among the play's critics, but Yeats courageously defended it and police removed the rowdy elements.

The play was toured with success in England, and 1907 also saw publication of a descriptive study, *The Aran Islands*. Synge's health was failing, however, and his wedding had to be postponed in 1908. He died in Dublin on 24 March 1909, and was buried at Mount Jerome cemetery. His *Poems and Translations* was published later in the year. *The Tinker's Wedding* was first performed in London in 1909, and *Deirdre of the Sorrows* at the Abbey in 1910.

See A plaque marks Synge's birthplace.
Read Robin Skelton, *J. M. Synge and his world* (Thames & Hudson, 1971).

(See plates 19 and 27)

—84— JACK B. YEATS

1871–1957 LITERARY PAINTER

Jack Butler Yeats was the youngest of the five children of the painter John B. Yeats. His father had barely finished art school when Yeats was born in London on 29 August 1871. Yeats spent much of his childhood with his mother's parents in Sligo, where he sketched with equal enthusiasm the town's quays and the dramatic landscapes of the surrounding countryside. Returning to London in 1887, he studied art and was soon contributing illustrations to such magazines as *The Vegetarian*, *Paddock Life* and *Lock to Lock Times*. Boxing and horseracing were favourite subjects, and many drawings were humorous.

In 1894, he married Mary Cottenham White, a Devon artist. In 1895, his water-colour of 'Strand Races, West of Ireland' was accepted by the Royal Hibernian Academy, and he gradually developed this side of his talent, since photography now threatened traditional illustrations. Paintings of the West – of tinkers, circus folk, jockeys and others known from childhood – increasingly dominated Yeats' exhibitions in Dublin and London.

Lady Gregory (*qv*) saw his work as complementing the Irish Literary Revival in which his brother W. B. Yeats (*qv*) was deeply involved. He illustrated articles by J. M. Synge (*qv*) on 'congested districts' in the West, and also his book on *The Aran Islands*. Other drawings accompanied broadsheet poems produced by the Cuala Press, and in 1912 he published *Life in the West of Ireland*.

Yeats and 'Cottie' moved from Devon to Greystones, Co Wicklow, in 1910, then to Dublin in 1917. He worked increasingly in oils, and paintings such as 'Bachelor's Walk: In Memory' (1915) and 'The Funeral of Harry Boland' (1922) reflected the unsettled times. As he grew older, the careful draughtmanship of Yeats' early work gave way to broader brushwork and richer colours, often with mystical titles such as 'A Race in Hy-Brazil' (1937) and 'And Graine saw this sun sink' (1950). His international reputation came late, but he soon outstripped all his Irish contemporaries.

Many Yeats paintings have a narrative element, and not surprisingly he turned to writing. *Sligo* (1930), *Ah Well* (1942) and *And to You Also* (1944) are reminiscences; his novels included *Sailing, Sailing Swiftly* (1933) and *The Aramanthers* (1936), and the Abbey Theatre staged such plays as *La La Noo* (1942) and *In Sand* (1949). None of his writing has the impact of his drawings and paintings, which are evocatively Irish. Yeats died in Dublin on 28 March 1957, and was buried in Mount Jerome cemetery.

See A plaque marks Yeats' home at 18 Fitzwilliam Sq, Dublin. His paintings are in the main Irish galleries.
Read Hilary Pyle, *Jack B. Yeats* (Routledge & Kegan Paul, 1970).

—85—
PATRICK GALLAGHER
1873–1966
'PADDY THE COPE'

Gallagher was born in a one-room cottage at Cleendra, in the Rosses district of Co Donegal, on 25 December 1873. He was one of nine children, and his father farmed a few acres of reclaimed bog overlooking the Atlantic Ocean. At ten, he was sent to the hiring fair at Strabane, Co Tyrone, and a nearby farmer paid him £3 for six months' work. Each spring, he hired to a different master, until at sixteen he went to Scotland, as his father had often done. He worked there and in England as farm labourer, builder and miner, always returning to Cleendra.

When Gallagher married, he took his wife to Scotland, but saved enough with a co-operative store to buy a farm at Cleendra; his new plough was the first in that barren district. In 1903, at a meeting in nearby Dungloe, he heard George Russell (*qv*) urge the formation of a co-operative agricultural bank, and became a member of its management committee. He soon had trouble with local merchants, when he tried to buy cheap fertiliser, and retaliated by creating the Templecrone Co-operative Society, aided by the Irish Agricultural Organisation Society founded by Sir Horace Plunkett (*qv*). The

IAOS confined itself to agricultural requirements, but Gallagher imported foodstuffs from Scotland.

Established traders, the 'gombeen men' who kept small farmers in debt to them, spread rumours that 'the Cope' in Dungloe was a unionist plot to divide the Catholic population, and when Gallagher was granted £300 to build a recreation hall, it was nicknamed 'the Orange hall'. He cunningly matched every trick, though he was once jailed for refusing to be put under rule of bail to be of good behaviour. After a friendly priest intervened, he was released by order of the lord justices in Dublin.

The War of Independence proved a dangerous time, and many co-operatives were burned by the Black and Tans. In 1921, the British Army blockaded the Rosses and the Gweedore district to the north, preventing provisions being sent by rail from Londonderry; Gallagher immediately chartered a steamer to bring food from Glasgow. In 1923, the co-operative built a pier at Dungloe, shipping products as diverse as knitwear and paving stones; the sight of a mill-wheel inspired Gallagher to build a power-house, providing free electricity to the main street and churches of Dungloe.

Russell frequently cited Templecrone as a good example to the whole country, and judged Gallagher a businessman of 'the type which is not infrequently born on an Irish bog and ends his days as an American millionaire'. After he had expressed a hope that 'Paddy the Cope' would leave his story behind him, Gallagher published *My Story* (1939), a simple and moving account of his struggles. He died at Dungloe on 24 June 1966.

—86—

SIR HUGH LANE

1875–1915
ART COLLECTOR

Lane was born on 9 November 1875 at Ballybrack, Co Cork, where his father was rector. His mother, Adelaide Persse, was a sister of Lady Gregory (*qv*), and she travelled extensively on the Continent with her young son. In 1893, he was apprenticed to the London art dealer, Martin Colnaghi, and in 1898 he opened his own small gallery in Pall Mall Place. Lane's flair for judging paintings, and for recognising the work of different artists, quickly made him a rich man.

In 1900, he visited his aunt at Coole Park, in Co Galway, meeting W. B. Yeats (*qv*) and others involved in the Irish Literary Revival. Conscious that there was no comparable art movement, Lane proposed a Dublin gallery to house modern works of art, both Irish and foreign. He commissioned John Butler Yeats, the poet's father, to paint leading Irish figures, and in 1904 staged in Dublin an exhibition of French paintings, many of which were bought for the proposed gallery.

Dublin Corporation then provided a temporary municipal gallery in Harcourt Street, which at its 1908 opening had paintings by Corot, Daumier, Degas, Millet and Constable. Lavery presented several paintings. He also lent thirty-nine paintings, mostly by French impressionists, promising to donate them when a permanent gallery had been established. He was knighted in 1909.

Lane asked Sir Edwin Lutyens to design a gallery, and the English architect proposed an imaginative building spanning the river Liffey below O'Connell Bridge. When Dublin Corporation decided against the scheme in 1913, Lane angrily removed his pictures from Harcourt Street. He altered his will, bequeathing them to the National Gallery in London, which meanwhile had them on loan. However, the London gallery was prepared to hang only a selection of Lane's paintings, and in 1914 his appointment as director of the National Gallery in Dublin helped to change his mind. In 1915, preparing for a visit to America, he added an unwitnessed codicil leaving the paintings to Dublin on condition that a suitable building was provided within five years of his death. He was drowned on 7 May 1915, when the *Lusitania* was torpedoed almost within sight of his birthplace.

Amid mounting controversy, Lady Gregory and others campaigned for Lane's pictures to return to Dublin. In 1924, a British parliamentary committee accepted the validity of the unwitnessed codicil but, since Dublin had not built a new gallery within five years, recommended that the pictures remain in London. In 1933, a permanent gallery was established in Parnell Square, but not until 1959 did the British and Irish governments reach an agreement to divide the collection into two groups, each being loaned to Dublin for alternating five-year periods. A revised agreement, giving Dublin more pictures, was concluded in 1979.

Visit The Hugh Lane Gallery, formerly the Municipal Gallery of Modern Art, Parnell Sq, Dublin.
Read Lady Gregory, *Sir Hugh Lane: His Life and Legacy* (Colin Smythe, Gerrards Cross, 1973).

—87—
JAMES LARKIN
1876–1947
'BIG JIM'

Larkin was born in Liverpool on 21 January 1876. The son of poor Irish emigrants, he spent his early years with grandparents in Newry, Co Down, before returning to Liverpool, where he worked from the age of nine. Eventually, he became a foreman docker, but lost his job for siding with his men in a strike. He then became an organiser for the National Union of Dock Labourers, commanding allegiance with mesmeric oratory.

In 1907, Larkin fought a lockout in Belfast docks, using new methods of 'blacking' goods and encouraging other workers to strike in sympathy, but his English-based union took fright at his militant methods. He moved to Dublin, where in 1909 he founded the Irish Transport and General Workers' Union. Larkin became its general secretary, recruiting thousands of members among the city's unskilled slum dwellers. Although he served three months in prison in 1910, on a charge of misusing union money, his popularity was undimmed.

In 1913, the principal Dublin employers determined to destroy Larkin's union. Their leader was William Martin Murphy, proprietor of the daily *Irish Independent* and director of the Dublin United Tramways Company, who demanded pledges of loyalty from his employees. The ITGWU retaliated by 'blacking' Murphy's newspapers and abandoning trams; soon, thousands of workers had been locked out by members of the employers' federation. Larkin was charged with seditious conspiracy, but evaded arrest until he appeared in disguise at a proscribed meeting in Sackville (now O'Connell) Street; a scuffle led to police baton charges, and two people were killed. Larkin was sentenced to seven months' imprisonment, but soon released when James Connolly (*qv*) closed the port of Dublin.

Although 'Big Jim' mustered aid from Great Britain, bringing food ships up the river Liffey, the strikers acknowledged defeat early in 1914. None the less, the ITGWU remained in existence, and the lockout had led to the formation of the Irish Citizen Army; under Connolly, the ICA would play its part in the 1916 rising. Meanwhile, Larkin set out for America in October 1914, hoping to raise funds, and did not return until 1923, having served almost three years in Sing Sing prison for 'criminal anarchy'.

The union had flourished in his absence, and after a legal action which bankrupted him Larkin was expelled in 1924. With his brother Peter, he then founded the Workers' Union of Ireland, gravely weakening the Labour movement as a political force; Larkin himself created the Irish Workers' League as a vehicle for his Marxism, and was active in international Communism. He became a Dublin city councillor, but was disqualified when first elected to the Dáil in 1927; he was later able to sit in the Dáil in 1937–8 and 1943–4. He died in Dublin on 30 January 1947, and was buried in Glasnevin cemetery.

See Statue by Oisín Kelly in O'Connell St, Dublin.
Read Emmet Larkin, *James Larkin, Irish Labour Leader, 1876–1947* (Routledge & Kegan Paul, 1965).

—88—
DANIEL CORKERY
1878–1964
CRITICAL INFLUENCE

Corkery was born at 1 Gardiners Hill, Cork, on 14 February 1878. He was educated at Presentation College, Cork, before training as a teacher at St Patrick's College, Dublin. Returning to Cork, he taught in national schools, where his pupils included Frank O'Connor (*qv*) and the sculptor Séamus Murphy. O'Connor and another writer of short stories, Seán O'Faoláin, were among those who gathered regularly at Corkery's house, finding the older man a stimulating if sometimes forbidding critic.

Corkery was in his late twenties when he taught himself Irish, and in 1908 he was a founder of the Cork Dramatic Society, for which he wrote plays in both languages. Another founder was his close friend Terence MacSwiney, who was to become lord mayor of Cork and die on hunger strike. Corkery was a competent water-colourist and came from a family of craftsmen in wood, so the theatre engaged his different talents. It was in the short story, however, that he set standards for other writers.

His first collection, *A Munster Twilight*, was published in 1916, and it was followed by *The Hounds of Banba* (1920), *The Stormy Hills* (1929) and *Earth out of Earth* (1939). With his novel, *The Threshold of Quiet* (1917), which draws on Thoreau's maxim about 'lives of quiet desperation', they provide a sombre portrait of Cork and its surroundings. Corkery was familiar with Russian literature, and the stories often recall Turgenev, but there is a narrow provincialism which has perhaps caused an unwarranted neglect.

In envisaging an Irish literature as powerful as Russian, Corkery believed it must derive from a particular allegiance to Ireland, and he was ready to dismiss Anglo-Irish contemporaries such as Somerville and Ross (*qqv*), who used the native Irish as comic relief. His classic work, *The Hidden Ireland* (1924), explored the rich Gaelic poetry of eighteenth-century Munster, romantically recalling a vanished civilisation. More controversial was his *Synge and Anglo-Irish Literature* (1931), whose polemical insights into Irish consciousness were vitiated by his unwillingness to acknowledge the real achievements of J. M. Synge (*qv*) and other Anglo-Irish writers. If his influence on Irish writing was profound, the best writers acknowledged and escaped from it.

In the 1920s, Corkery taught art and became a schools inspector and organiser in the Irish language, before being appointed, in 1931, professor of English at University College, Cork. He retired in 1947, and became a senator in 1951–4. His last book was *The Fortunes of the Irish Language* (1954). Unmarried, he died at Passage West, Co Cork, on 31 December 1964.

Read G. Brandon Saul, *Daniel Corkery* (Bucknell University Press, Lewisburg, 1973).

—89—
OLIVER ST JOHN GOGARTY
1878–1957
MANY-SIDED MAN

Gogarty, son of a wealthy Catholic physician, was born at 5 Rutland (now Parnell) Square, Dublin, on 17 August 1878. Educated in England and at Clongowes Wood, the Jesuit college in Co Kildare, he played professional football for Preston and won an Irish cup medal with the Bohemians club. While studying medicine at Trinity College, Dublin, he was an Irish champion racing cyclist. In 1904, he spent a few weeks with James Joyce (*qv*) at the Martello tower in Sandycove, Co Dublin, and unwillingly became 'stately, plump Buck Mulligan' in Joyce's *Ulysses.*

Gogarty won the vice-chancellor's verse prize at Trinity College but in two terms at Oxford University failed to emulate the success of Oscar Wilde (*qv*) in the Newdigate Prize. In 1905, he spoke at Sinn Féin's first convention, and wrote regularly for *The United Irishman*; Arthur Griffith (*qv*), before his death in 1922, considered Gogarty might become the Irish Free State's first governor-general. In 1906, Gogarty married Martha Duane of Moyard, Co Galway, and they spent a year in Vienna after his graduation in 1907.

Back in Dublin, Gogarty quickly established a reputation as a surgeon, and hosted fashionable evenings at his home in Ely Place. He was one of a small group who, in the Bailey restaurant in Duke Street, produced the best conversation in Dublin. It was said they would 'sacrifice their mother for a witty phrase', and Gogarty rarely curbed his tongue. On the death of the painter William Orpen, he commented 'He never got under the surface till he got under the sod.' When an operation went wrong and an assistant called out 'Jesus Christ', Gogarty retorted 'Cease calling on your unqualified assistant.'

In 1917, his play *Blight* at the Abbey Theatre antedated O'Casey (*qv*) in attacking Dublin's slums; in 1919, *A Serious Thing* satirised British rule in Ireland. During the War of Independence, Gogarty provided a 'safe house' for Michael Collins (*qv*), and took part in a jailbreak. In 1923, a member of the new Senate, he was captured by republicans; he escaped assassination by throwing himself into the river Liffey, and in gratitude presented two swans to 'the goddess of the river'. His beloved country home at Renvyle, Co Galway, was burned down, but he rebuilt and reopened it as a hotel. In 1924, he organised the Taillteann Games, reviving an ancient tradition; he came third in archery, and won a gold medal for his book of verse, *An Offering of Swans*. A pioneer of civil aviation, he helped to form the Irish Aero Club in 1928.

Gogarty turned increasingly from medicine to literature, publishing his memoirs in *As I Was Going Down Sackville Street* (1936), *Tumbling in the Hay* (1939) and *It Isn't This Time of Year at All* (1954). The first occasioned a libel action, which Gogarty lost; disliking the bourgeois Ireland of Eamon de Valera (*qv*), he left Dublin in 1937 to practise in London. He spent World War II in America, and thereafter his visits to Ireland were brief. He died in New York on 22 September 1957.

See A plaque marks Gogarty's birthplace.
Read Ulick O'Connor, *Oliver St John Gogarty: A Poet and his Times* (Cape, 1964).

—90—

PATRICK PEARSE

1879–1916
BLOOD SACRIFICE

Patrick Henry Pearse (Pádraic or Pádraig Mac Piarais) was born on 10 November 1879 at 27 Great Brunswick (now Pearse) Street, Dublin. His father was an English stonemason drawn to Dublin by the churchbuilding which followed Catholic emancipation; his mother came from Co Meath. Pearse developed a love of the Irish language at the Christian Brothers school in Westland Row, and in 1896 joined the Gaelic League, soon becoming a member of its executive.

He graduated from the Royal University in 1901, and was called to the Bar, but he seldom practised. Instead, he helped his younger brother Willie run the family business and he taught Irish at University College, Dublin. In 1903, Pearse became editor of the Gaelic League journal, *An Claidheamh Soluis*.

In 1908, Pearse opened a bilingual school for boys in the Dublin suburb of Rathmines, naming it St Enda's after the patron saint of the Aran Islands. Sited in a Georgian mansion, it was adorned by the work of artists such as Sarah Purser, George Russell and Jack B. Yeats (*qqv*); one fresco incorporated words attributed to the legendary Cuchulainn, 'I care not though I were to live but one day and one night provided my fame and my deeds live after me.'

In 1910, Pearse moved to larger premises at The Hermitage, Rathfarnham, where Robert Emmet (*qv*) had courted Sarah Curran; his first school became St Ita's, accommodating girls. He had overreached himself financially, however, and the teaching suffered. He managed to keep St Enda's going, but not St Ita's.

Now engrossed in the writings of Wolfe Tone and John Mitchel (*qqv*), Pearse delivered a notable oration at the Emmet commemoration meeting in 1911. He envisaged himself dying in an Irish revolution. In November 1913, he joined with Eoin MacNeill (*qv*) and others to form the Irish Volunteers; a month later, he joined the secret Irish Republican Brotherhood. In 1915, Pearse delivered a famous oration at the burial of the old Fenian, O'Donovan Rossa, ending 'the fools, the fools, the fools, they have left us our Fenian dead, and while Ireland holds these graves Ireland unfree shall never be at peace'.

When the Easter Rising began on 24 April 1916, Pearse read the proclamation of the Irish Republic to unreceptive bystanders outside the General Post Office in Sackville (now O'Connell) Street, Dublin. He became president of the provisional government and commander-in-chief of the republican army. Five days later, Pearse agreed to an unconditional surrender. On 3 May 1916, following a court-martial, he was executed by a firing squad in Kilmainham Jail. Willie Pearse was one of fourteen others shot dead. The blood sacrifice had been made.

Visit St Enda's, Grange Rd, Rathfarnham, is now a Pearse museum; nature walk in grounds (guidebook; open daily). Kilmainham Jail museum, Dublin (open Sun afternoons). Pearse's summer cottage, near Rosmuc (8½ miles/13.5 km S of Maam Cross, Co Galway) is a national monument.

Read Hedley McCay, *Padraic Pearse* (Mercier Press, Cork, 1966); Ruth Dudley Edwards, *Patrick Pearse: The Triumph of Failure* (Gollancz, 1977).

—91—
SEÁN O'CASEY
1880–1964
'THE GREEN CROW'

John Casey, as he was christened, was born at 85 Upper Dorset Street, Dublin, on 30 March 1880. His father, a tenement caretaker, died in 1886. The boy suffered poor health, and trachoma impaired his eyesight. None the less, although he attended a Protestant church school only irregularly, he was a prolific reader and learned extensive Bible passages from his devout mother. He also acted in plays with an elder brother, and performed *The Shaughraun* by Dion Boucicault (*qv*) in what later became the Abbey Theatre.

He became a railway labourer, and in 1911 joined the Irish Transport and General Workers' Union formed by James Larkin (*qv*); much of his early writing was for Larkin's *Irish Worker*. He had joined the Gaelic League as Seán Ó Cathasaigh, and belonged for a time to the Irish Republican Brotherhood; in 1914, he became briefly secretary to the Irish Citizen Army. An opinionated and combative figure, O'Casey gave his loyalty to socialism (in later years, he became a committed if idiosyncratic Communist) rather than republicanism, and he took no part in the 1916 rising, save to be briefly detained. When he published *The Story of the Irish Citizen Army* (1919), it was ill received.

By then he was submitting plays to the Abbey; when W. B. Yeats (*qv*) advised him to write of life as he knew it, the outcome was *The Shadow of a Gunman* (1923). The semi-autobiographical play, set in Dublin's slums and dealing with the recent War of Independence, was an immediate success. In 1924, O'Casey confirmed his promise with *Juno and the Paycock*, a tragi-comedy depicting the 'turrible state of chassis' in the recent Civil War. The last of O'Casey's great trilogy, *The Plough and the Stars*, opened on 8 February 1926. On the fourth night, rioting broke out, the demonstrators unjustly condemning the play as an insult to the heroes of 1916. Yeats, recalling earlier hostility towards J. M. Synge (*qv*), told the audience they had 'disgraced yourselves again. Is this to be the ever recurring celebration of the arrival of Irish genius?'

The following month, disillusioned by acrimonious public debate, O'Casey went to London to receive the Hawthornden Prize for *Juno and the Paycock*. He remained there, marrying the Irish actress Eileen Carey, and wrote *The Silver Tassie*, depicting the horrors of World War I. Yeats thought it a bad play, the Abbey rejected it, and in 1929 it lost money in a London run. The embittered O'Casey was eventually reconciled with Yeats, and the Abbey staged *The Silver Tassie* in 1935, but by then his work had lost its early force and the new bourgeois Ireland no longer inspired him. Later plays included *Red Roses for Me* (published in 1943), *Purple Dust* (1945), *Cock-a-Doodle-Dandy* (1949), *The Bishop's Bonfire* (1955) and *The Drums of Father Ned* (1959). None moved audiences as the Abbey trilogy had done, or added to the theatrical pantheon characters as memorable as Joxer Daly and Fluther Good.

O'Casey published six volumes of semi-fictional autobiography between 1939 and 1954. His hostility to Ireland provoked many critics there, and they found his books anti-clerical. After 1936, the 'Green Crow' (as he called himself) rarely visited Ireland. In 1938, he and his family moved to Devon, where they could live cheaply, and he died at Torquay on 18 September 1964.

See A plaque on the Hibernian Bank marks the site of O'Casey's birthplace.

Read David Krause, *Seán O'Casey and his world* (Thames & Hudson, 1976); Hugh Hunt, *Seán O'Casey* (Gill & Macmillan, Dublin, 1980).

(See plates 19 and 28)

—92—

WILLIAM T. COSGRAVE

1880–1965
THE QUIET MAN

Cosgrave was born at 174 James's Street, Dublin, on 6 June 1880. His father, a publican, was a city councillor and poor law guardian, so he grew up in a political environment. Educated at Christian Brothers schools, he entered his father's business. In 1905, Cosgrave attended the first Sinn Féin convention, and in 1909 he was elected to Dublin Corporation, remaining a councillor for most of the period to 1922. He joined the Irish Volunteers in 1913, and in 1916 served under Eamonn Ceannt in the heavy fighting that accompanied the seizure of the South Dublin Union. His subsequent death sentence was commuted to penal servitude for life.

Released under the 1917 amnesty, Cosgrave soon won a parliamentary by-election in Kilkenny City, and was unopposed in the 1918 general election. As treasurer of Sinn Féin, he was rearrested soon afterwards, but on his release in 1919 became minister for local government in the First Dáil. Although on the run, he did much to undermine the existing institutions of local government, particularly after Sinn Féin swept the 1920 council elections everywhere but in Ulster.

Cosgrave supported the 1921 Anglo-Irish Treaty and, after the sudden deaths of Arthur Griffith and Michael Collins (*qqv*), became chairman of the provisional government and then president of the executive council (ie prime minister) of the new Irish Free State. A quiet and undemonstrative leader, Cosgrave held this post until 1932; he also held for a time the portfolios in finance and defence, the latter following a threatened army mutiny in 1924. By the time he was defeated by Eamon de Valera (*qv*) in the 1932 election, he had established a secure parliamentary democracy and had achieved in dominion status a cordial and almost complete independence from the United Kingdom.

He continued to lead Cumann na nGaedheal (as his party had become in 1923) in opposition. When it merged with other parties in 1933 to become Fine Gael (Tribe of Gaels), Gen Eoin O'Duffy was elected president; he had been dismissed as commissioner of police by de Valera, and his Blueshirt movement briefly threatened the country's stability until he resigned and was succeeded by the level-headed Cosgrave. The latter remained opposition leader until he resigned from the Dáil in 1944. He became a member of the Irish Racing Board in 1945, and was its chairman for many years. Cosgrave died in Dublin on 16 November 1965.

See A plaque marks Cosgrave's birthplace.

—93—
JAMES JOYCE
1882–1941
PORTRAIT OF THE ARTIST

Joyce was born at 41 Brighton Square, Rathgar, Dublin, on 2 February 1882. His father invested unwisely, and the family's fortunes declined steadily. In 1888, Joyce was sent to Clongowes Wood, the Jesuit college in Co Kildare, but was withdrawn when his father lost his job as a rates collector. The family moved into lodgings on the poorer north side of Dublin, and Joyce was taught by Christian Brothers before returning to Jesuits at Belvedere College in 1893.

Joyce won several scholastic prizes, and had periods of religious fervour, but an encounter with a prostitute beside the Grand Canal had introduced him at fourteen to other pleasures, and his religious faith slowly dissipated. Soon after graduating from University College, Dublin, in 1902 he embarked impractically on medical studies at the Sorbonne in Paris. His mother's impending death brought him back to Dublin.

In 1904, Joyce began *Stephen Hero*, the unfinished novel which he later reworked as *A Portrait of the Artist as a Young Man*. He wrote some stories for *The Irish Homestead*, edited by George Russell (*qv*), which later appeared in *Dubliners*. He also met a chambermaid called Nora Barnacle, and on 16 June 1904 they went walking at Ringsend, at the Liffey's mouth; Joyce was to choose that date for the events recorded in *Ulysses*. Later in the summer, he briefly shared a Martello tower at Sandycove, Co Dublin, with Oliver St John Gogarty (*qv*).

In October 1904, Joyce and Nora sailed from Dublin. Joyce found employment in a language school in Trieste, where he was joined in 1905 by his brother Stanislaus. In 1907, a book of poems, *Chamber Music*, was published in London. Joyce made two trips to Dublin in 1909, to arrange publication of *Dubliners* and to open a short-lived cinema. His last visit was in 1912, when he failed to overcome his publisher's doubts about *Dubliners*.

In 1914, *A Portrait* was serialised in the London magazine, *The Egoist*, and *Dubliners* found a London publisher. With the outbreak of World War I, Stanislaus was interned but Joyce was allowed to travel to Zurich in neutral Switzerland, where in 1917 he underwent the first of many eye operations after an attack of glaucoma. *Ulysses*, his masterpiece, was serialised in *The Little Review* in New York in 1918–20, but was eventually halted by a court action; *Exiles*, a play, was published in 1918.

Joyce returned to Trieste in 1919, but moved to Paris the following year, and in 1922 *Ulysses* was published there by Sylvia Beach, American owner of a celebrated bookshop. Joyce's portrait of a Dublin remembered in fine detail, and of the odyssey of the Jewish advertisement canvasser Leopold Bloom, revolutionised the novel with its 'stream of consciousness' technique. In 1923, Joyce began *Finnegans Wake*, an almost impenetrable linguistic comedy published in 1939. In 1927, Sylvia Beach published his later poems as *Pomes Penyeach*. *Ulysses* was published in America in 1934, after it was ruled not to be pornographic, and a British edition followed in 1936. Joyce and Nora had finally married in 1931, and in 1940 they returned to Zurich, where Joyce died on 13 January 1941.

Visit James Joyce Tower, Sandycove, Co Dublin, contains interesting Joyceana (open May–Sept, Mon–Sat and Sun afternoons; guidebook). Joyce centre at 35 North Great George's St, Dublin.
See Bust by Marjorie Fitzgibbon in St Stephen's Green, Dublin.
Read Chester G. Anderson, *James Joyce and his world* (Thames & Hudson, 1967), Peter Costello, *James Joyce* (Gill & Macmillan, Dublin, 1980).

(See plate 29)

—94—
EAMON DE VALERA
1882–1975
'DEV'

De Valera was born in New York on 14 October 1882. His Spanish father died in 1885, and his widowed mother sent him to his grandmother's cottage at Bruree, Co Limerick. He won a scholarship to Blackrock College, Dublin, then completed his degree in the Royal University in 1904. By then, he was teaching mathematics at Rockwell College, near Cashel, Co Tipperary. He later held teaching posts in the Dublin area, and in 1910 married Sinéad Flanagan, who had taught him Irish.

Baptised Edward, he became Eamon after joining the Gaelic League in 1908. He joined the Irish Volunteers in 1913, and the Irish Republican Brotherhood in 1915. During the 1916 rising, he commanded the garrison at Boland's Mills; his death sentence was commuted, and he was released in 1917. The most senior survivor of the rising, he was elected MP for East Clare in a by-election. Having left the IRB, he succeeded Arthur Griffith (*qv*) as president of Sinn Féin in 1917, and also became president of the Volunteers.

In 1918, de Valera was interned in England. Escaping from Lincoln jail in 1919, he was elected president of Dáil Éireann, the separatist assembly of Sinn Féin MPs. As the War of Independence spread, he visited America to raise money for the Dáil, but failed in efforts to raise the Irish problem at the Versailles peace conference. A truce was negotiated in July 1921, and the Anglo-Irish Treaty was signed in London in December; Ireland had now been partitioned, and a Unionist government controlled six Ulster counties.

De Valera had left the treaty negotiations to Griffith and Michael Collins (*qv*), who had not persuaded the British to accept his formula for 'external association' with the United Kingdom. He unsuccessfully argued that the Dáil should reject the treaty, criticising principally the oath of allegiance to the crown, and resigned the presidency. As Ireland drifted into the Civil War, he enlisted as a private in his old battalion of Volunteers, now the Irish Republican Army. He formed a rival government, but eventually persuaded the IRA to give up its unequal struggle against the Irish Free State in May 1923.

In 1926, de Valera broke with Sinn Féin to form Fianna Fáil (Warriors of Destiny); its Dáil representatives made it clear they did not consider the oath of allegiance binding. In 1932, Fianna Fáil became the largest party, and de Valera formed an administration, holding office until 1948. The oath was abolished in 1933; in 1936, he exploited the British abdication crisis to pass an External Relations Act which largely abolished the crown's role. A new constitution followed in 1937, reflecting Catholic social policy as much as republicanism; the state was renamed Éire or Ireland, with de Valera as taoiseach or prime minister. A wave of murders in 1936 led him to proscribe the IRA.

During World War II, de Valera maintained Irish neutrality, and in 1941 successfully protested against a proposal to extend British conscription to Northern Ireland. He interned more than a thousand members of the IRA, and in 1941 sent Dublin's fire-engines to Belfast when the northern city was bombed. In 1945, he met Winston Churchill's criticism of Irish neutrality by reminding him of 'a small nation that stood alone not for a year or two, but for several hundred years against aggression'.

Defeated in 1948, 'Dev' again held office in 1951–4 and 1957–9, despite failing eyesight. Elected president of Ireland in 1959, he served two seven-year terms. He died in Dublin on 29 August 1975. Although he had failed in two principal objectives, to end partition and to revive the Irish language, he had proved an enduring statesman. 'Whenever I wanted to know what the Irish people wanted,' he said during the 1921 treaty debate, 'I had only to examine my own heart.'

Visit Aras de Valera Museum, Bruree, Co Limerick.
See Statue in Ennis, Co Clare.
Read The Earl of Longford & Thomas P. O'Neill, *Eamon de Valera* (Hutchinson, 1970); T. Ryle Dwyer, *Eamon de Valera* (Gill & Macmillan, Dublin, 1980).

—95— HARRY FERGUSON

1884–1960
A LONELY FURROW

Ferguson was born at Growell, near Hillsborough, Co Down, on 4 November 1884. He left school at fourteen but, being slight of build, was ill-suited to work on the family farm; moreover, Ferguson found his father's authoritarian Protestantism inimical to his own instinctive curiosity. In 1902, he joined his brother Joe, who had opened a car and bicycle repair business in Belfast. His aptitude for tuning engines helped the business prosper, and in 1904 he began to race motor-cycles. In 1909, at Hillsborough, he made the first powered flight in Ireland, travelling 130 yd (118.5 m) in a monoplane he had himself built. He later drove racing cars, and helped to establish the famous Ulster Tourist Trophy races in 1928.

Never at ease in a subordinate role, Ferguson set up his own motor business in 1911. During World War I, he began to demonstrate and sell tractors to Irish farmers accustomed to horse-drawn ploughs. He soon conceived what was then a revolutionary concept, that tractor and plough should be designed as a unit. Over the next few years, Ferguson developed his ideas and registered patents; when the American tycoon, Henry Ford, offered a job the Ulsterman preferred his independence and set up an American company to manufacture Ferguson ploughs. In 1926, the principal patent of the Ferguson system – hydraulic regulation of the working depth of the various implements linked to the tractor – was granted. In time, the system changed the face of agriculture, but commercial success proved initially elusive.

Ferguson eventually turned to Henry Ford, and in 1938 demonstrated his manoeuvrable lightweight tractor at Dearborn, Michigan. Ford offered to buy the patents, but Ferguson offered instead a 'gentlemen's agreement' by which the American could manufacture the tractor for Ferguson to sell, and the deal was sealed only by a handshake. The Ford/Ferguson tractor contributed enormously to wartime food production, but the idealistic Ulsterman's real hope was to raise living standards throughout the world. 'Agriculture,' he said in 1943, 'should have been the first industry to be modernised and not the last.'

In 1946, after Henry Ford had died and his grandson repudiated the gentlemen's agreement, Ferguson was forced to build his own assembly plant at Detroit. In 1948, he sued the Ford Motor Company for $251m for conspiring to destroy his business and for non-payment of royalties, and in 1952 Fords agreed to pay $9.25m in compensation. A 1953 merger with the Canadian Massey-Harris concern worked out unhappily for Ferguson, and he retired to his country home at Stow-on-the Wold, in Gloucestershire. His final ambition was to improve car safety through a four-wheel drive system and anti-lock braking, but he failed to make a commercial breakthrough. He suffered from insomnia and depression and, when he died from a drugs overdose on 25 October 1960, a coroner's jury returned an open verdict.

Read Colin Fraser, *Harry Ferguson: Inventor and Pioneer* (Murray, 1972).

—96—
MICHAEL COLLINS
1890–1922
'THE BIG FELLOW'

Collins, son of a small farmer, was born near Sam's Cross, Clonakilty, Co Cork, on 16 October 1890. Educated locally, he became a post office clerk in 1906. Sent to London, he learned Irish at Gaelic League classes, and joined Sinn Féin. He joined the Irish Republican Brotherhood in 1909 and, in 1914, a company of Irish Volunteers. He returned to Ireland in January 1916, to avoid conscription in England.

During the Easter Rising, Collins fought in the General Post Office. He was interned at Stafford, in England, then at Frongoch, in Wales, using the time to study and organise. Released in December 1916, he was appointed secretary of a republican relief organisation, and became a member of the IRB supreme council. He was active in Sinn Féin, and became director of organisation in the reviving Volunteer movement.

When de Valera, Cosgrave (*qqv*) and other republican leaders were arrested in 1918, Collins eluded the police. Thereafter he was on the run, organising for insurrection and building up a remarkable intelligence system. Elected MP for South Cork in 1918, he became minister for home affairs in the First Dáil, but he missed the historic first meeting, for he was preparing de Valera's escape from Lincoln jail. Collins later became finance minister under de Valera, raising substantial loans for Sinn Féin, director of intelligence in the Volunteers, and president of the IRB supreme council.

In the ensuing guerilla warfare, Collins' special squad systematically assassinated members of the 'G' division of the Dublin Metropolitan Police, Dublin Castle's main source of intelligence; he had his own informants at detective headquarters. 'The Big Fellow' worked from a number of offices, slept in 'safe houses' and went undisguised through Dublin. On the 'Bloody Sunday' of 21 November 1920, his men shot dead eleven British intelligence officers in the city, including the 'Cairo Gang' recruited to track Collins down. In retaliation, British Black and Tans killed fourteen people at a football game; Collins' family home in Co Cork was burned out in April 1921.

Collins was a reluctant negotiator and signatory of the 1921 Anglo-Irish Treaty, and wrote to a friend 'early this morning I signed my death warrant'. In the subsequent Dáil debate, he argued that the treaty 'gives us freedom, not the ultimate freedom that all nations desire and develop to, but the freedom to achieve it'. Collins became chairman of the provisional government which preceded the Irish Free State, and Dublin Castle was surrendered to him. On the outbreak of the Civil War in June 1922, he became commander-in-chief of the forces loyal to the government. On 22 August 1922, ten days after the death of Arthur Griffith (*qv*), he was ambushed and shot dead at Béal na mBláth, Co Cork. He was buried in Glasnevin cemetery, Dublin.

See Memorials at Sam's Cross ($4\frac{1}{4}$ miles/7 km WSW of Clonakilty) by Séamus Murphy; at Béal na mBláth (2 miles/3 km SW of Crookstown, Co Cork); and at Leinster Lawn, Merrion Sq, Dublin,

with portrait medallion by Laurence Campbell.
Read Margery Forester, *Michael Collins – The Lost Leader* (Sidgwick & Jackson, 1971); Leon Ó Broin, *Michael Collins* (Gill & Macmillan, Dublin, 1980).

(See plate 30)

—97— SEAN LEMASS

1899–1971 MAKER OF MODERN IRELAND

Lemass was born at Ballybrack, Co Dublin, on 15 July 1899. His father was a draper in Capel Street, Dublin, and an active supporter of the Irish parliamentary party. Lemass was educated at Christian Brothers schools in the city; he was fifteen, but looked older, when he joined the Irish Volunteers. When the Easter Rising began in 1916, he joined the occupiers of the General Post Office; because of his youth, he was released soon after the surrender, and rose steadily in the ranks of the Volunteers. Active in the War of Independence, he was arrested in December 1920 and interned for a year at Ballykinler, Co Down.

Opposed to the 1921 Anglo-Irish Treaty, Lemass was second-in-command when anti-Treaty members of the Irish Republican Army occupied the Four Courts in Dublin in 1922. After the garrison surrendered, he escaped to fight in the Civil War, but was later captured and interned. In 1924, he was elected to the Dáil as Sinn Féin member for a Dublin constituency, but did not take his seat. When Eamon de Valera (*qv*) formed the Fianna Fáil party in 1926, Lemass became its secretary and creator of a formidable political machine. In 1932, he became minister for industry and commerce in the first Fianna Fáil administration; apart from brief periods of opposition, he held this post until 1959. In 1945, he became tánaiste (deputy prime minister).

During the 1930s, Lemass favoured protective tariffs, and new industries arose to serve the Irish market. He established large public enterprises such as Aer Lingus and the peat-exploiting Bord na Móna. With the Irish Free State neutral in World War II, he also became minister for supplies. In 1959, Lemass succeeded de Valera as taoiseach, and pursued a vigorous policy of economic expansion, encouraging large-scale foreign investment. In 1965, he concluded a free trade agreement with the United Kingdom, in preparation for Ireland's entry into the European Economic Community, and by his pragmatism increasingly turned an inward-looking country into one with international horizons and a new self-confidence. He courageously visited the prime minister of Northern Ireland, Capt Terence O'Neill, in an attempt to improve relations between the two parts of Ireland.

Lemass resigned from office in 1966, and left the Dáil in 1969. He had set up a committee to consider revisions in the 1937 Irish constitution, and became a member of it. He also became chairman or director of many Irish companies, indulging a taste for business which had been suppressed during his political career, save that he managed his country like an ambitious entrepreneur. He died in Dublin on 11 May 1971.

—98—

MICHEÁL MAC LIAMMÓIR

1899–1978
PLAYER KING

Mac Liammóir was born in Cork on 25 October 1899. His family moved to London, and he became a child actor at the Little Theatre in 1911, taking a number of West End roles during the next four years. In 1915–16, he studied at the Slade School of Art, and subsequently designed for Edward Martyn's Irish Theatre and the Dublin Drama League. He spent several years painting in Europe before returning to Ireland in 1927 to join Anew McMaster's touring company, performing Shakespeare by oil lamp on makeshift stages.

Mac Liammóir had joined the Gaelic League in London, and was a fluent Irish speaker. In August 1928, he directed his own play, *Diarmuid agus Gráinne*, at the opening of the Taibhdearc na Gaillimhe, a government-subsidised Gaelic theatre in Galway.

Two months later, he and Hilton Edwards, an Englishman who was to be his lifelong associate, opened the Gate Theatre in Dublin. They began in the tiny Peacock Theatre, an annexe of the Abbey, staging *Peer Gynt* with a cast of 48 before a capacity audience of 102.

In 1930, the Gate found a larger, permanent home in Parnell Square, and a remarkable benefactor in the 6th Earl of Longford. In 1936, he formed the separate Longford Players, sharing the theatre with the Gate Company; each toured for part of the year, and Mac Liammóir played in Egypt and the Balkans before World War II. The Abbey had declined into kitchen comedy, and Mac Liammóir and Edwards set new standards of professionalism in a wide range of international drama. Mac Liammóir himself had all the theatrical talents: he was actor, director, playwright, designer of sets and costumes, and able to translate from several languages.

In 1947, he starred in his own *Ill Met by Moonlight* in London, then made his New York debut in *John Bull's Other Island* in 1948. In 1949, he played Iago in the film *Othello*, directed by Orson Welles, who had begun his career at the Gate. Mac Liammóir's amusing diary of the production was published as *Put Money in Thy Purse* (1952). Other memoirs included *All for Hecuba* (1946), *Each Actor on His Ass* (1960) and *Enter a Goldfish* (1977).

His 1932 Hamlet was possibly his finest performance, but his greatest theatrical success came in 1960, when he launched his one-man entertainment, *The Importance of Being Oscar*. His portrayal of Oscar Wilde (*qv*) captivated audiences throughout the world; in 1975, his last stage appearance was his 1384th as Oscar, appropriately at the Gate. He had survived a stroke and his sight was failing, but his theatrical flair and courage were undimmed. He died in Dublin on 6 March 1978.

See A plaque marks 4 Harcourt Terrace, Dublin, the Regency house Mac Liammóir shared with Edwards (1903–1982).

—99—

FRANK O'CONNOR

1903–1966
STORYTELLER

O'Connor's real name was Michael O'Donovan. He was born in Cork on 17 September 1903. His father, a labourer given to bouts of drunkenness, had been a bandsman in the British Army; his mother (*née* O'Connor), to whom he was deeply attached, had been brought up in the Good Shepherd orphanage. At school, he was taught for a time by Daniel Corkery (*qv*), who introduced him to the Irish language. At fourteen, he became a railway clerk, then got caught up in the War of Independence as an IRA volunteer. 'My fight for Irish freedom was of the same order as my fight for other sorts of freedom,' he recalled. 'I went a bit of the way with everybody, and in those days everybody was moving in the same direction.' He was also a member of Corkery's literary group, reading widely and educating himself.

He took the republican side in the Civil War, and was captured in 1923. During his internment, he found the 'sentimental highmindedness' of republicanism accompanied by an 'extraordinary inhumanity', and he became unpopular for refusing to join a hunger strike. On release, he became a librarian, working successively in Sligo, Wicklow and Cork. By now, he had begun to publish short stories under his pen-name, and was friendly with George Russell and W. B. Yeats (*qqv*); he formed a dramatic society in Cork, but found the city suffocatingly provincial and in 1928 took a Dublin post.

A collection of stories drawn from his IRA days, *Guests of the Nation*, was published in 1931; the title story describes the futile reprisal killing of two British soldiers. Although he published two novels, *The Saint and Mary Kate* (1932) and *Dutch Interior* (1940), his international reputation has rested in the masterly economy of stories collected under such titles as *Bones of Contention* (1936) and *Crab Apple Jelly* (1944).

In 1935, O'Connor became a director of Dublin's Abbey

Theatre, but resigned after Yeats' death in 1939, partly to concentrate on writing (he had also left the library) but also because he was unwilling to continue battling the 'Catholic–Nationalist establishment' which he felt was spoiling the theatre. Two of his plays were produced at the Abbey, *In the Train* (1937) and *Moses' Rock* (1938).

O'Connor's other writing included two volumes of autobiography, *The Big Fellow* (1937) – a study of Michael Collins (*qv*), critical works such as *The Lonely Voice* (1963) and translations of Irish poetry, notably *The Midnight Court* (1945) by Brian Merriman (*qv*). From 1939 onwards, he taught in American universities, returning to Ireland in 1960. He died on 10 March 1966.

See A plaque marks O'Connor's final home, Court Flats, Wilton Place, Dublin. The childhood homes recalled in his books are 251 Blarney St (now demolished) and 9 Harrington Sq, Cork.
Read Frank O'Connor, *An Only Child* (Macmillan, 1961) and *My Father's Son* (Gill & Macmillan, Dublin, 1968), covering his life to 1923 and 1939 respectively; the latter includes vivid portraits of Russell, Yeats and other literary figures.

—100—
PATRICK KAVANAGH
1904–1967
'THE GREEN FOOL'

Kavanagh was born near Inniskeen, Co Monaghan, on 21 October 1904. He was the elder son of the village shoemaker, and at fourteen was apprenticed to the same trade, helping also to work his father's few acres of land. He was to write later of the 'barbaric life of the Irish country poor', and the stony, grey soil of Monaghan made an indelible impression. Kavanagh was no scholar at the local school – 'I grabbed an education late but barely' – but he wrote poetry from his boyhood and in 1928 a weekly newspaper published his verse. The following year, George Russell (*qv*) published his work in *The Irish Statesman*; Kavanagh visited him in Dublin in 1930, returning with a pile of books from Russell's library.

In 1936, *Ploughman and Other Poems* was published in London, and Kavanagh moved briefly to England to begin his semi-fictional autobiography. *The Green Fool* was completed in Inniskeen and published in 1938, provoking a libel action by Oliver St John Gogarty (*qv*). Gogarty was awarded £100 damages for a passage in which Kavanagh wrote 'I mistook Gogarty's white-robed maid for his wife – or his mistress. I expected every poet to have a spare wife.'

In 1939, Kavanagh made 'the mistake of my life' and moved to Dublin. He knew his inspiration lay in the small world around Inniskeen, in a favourite bush or a group of stepping stones, though he was later to write lyrically and as precisely of the Dublin around Baggot Street Bridge and the Grand Canal. His long and bitter poem of rural life, *The Great Hunger* (1942), established his claim to be a major poet; subsequent collections included *A Soul for Sale* (1947) and *Come Dance with Kitty Stobling* (1960). Kavanagh matured from a tragic to a comic view of life; he was a sharp satirist of 'malignant Dublin', but his 'canal bank' poems show a detached acceptance of God and nature. His novel, *Tarry Flynn* (1948), reflected a mellower view of the Irish countryside.

In 1952, Kavanagh and his brother Peter published sixteen issues of *Kavanagh's Weekly*, an outspoken literary and political journal. He also embarked on an unsuccessful libel action in 1954, suing a Dublin weekly, *The Leader*, over an unflattering profile. Always an acerbic figure in Dublin's literary world, he suffered ill health in later years, and underwent a lung cancer operation in 1955. He married shortly before his death on 30 November 1967.

Visit Inniskeen (4 miles/6 km NNW of Louth) contains many reminders of Kavanagh, including a small museum. His birthplace is signposted, and in the graveyard a modern cross is inscribed 'And pray for him who walked apart on the hills loving life's miracles'.
See A plaque marks 62 Pembroke Rd, Dublin, where Kavanagh lived 1943–58. A commemorative seat at Baggot Street Bridge, recalling his lines 'O commemorate me where there is water, Canal water preferably, so stilly Greeny at the heart of summer'.
Read Peter Kavanagh, *Patrick Kavanagh Country* (Goldsmith Press, The Curragh, Ireland, 1978).

(See plate 31).

DATES IN IRISH HISTORY

432 St Patrick's mission to Ireland
795 Viking raids on Ireland begin
1014 Brian Boru defeats Vikings at Clontarf
1169 Norman invasion of Ireland
1494 Poyning's Law subordinates Irish parliament to English rule
1586 Plantation of Munster
1591 Foundation of Trinity College, Dublin (Dublin University)
1598 Battle of the Yellow Ford: victory for Hugh O'Neill
1601 Battle of Kinsale: O'Neill defeated
1607 Flight of the Earls
1609 Plantation of Ulster
1641 Irish rebellion
1646 Battle of Benburb: victory for Owen Roe O'Neill
1649 Oliver Cromwell in Ireland
1681 Oliver Plunkett executed in London
1689 Siege of Londonderry
1690 Battle of the Boyne: William III defeats James II
1691 Treaty of Limerick
1695 Beginning of penal laws against Catholics
1724 Jonathan Swift's *Drapier's Letters*
1782 Irish parliamentary independence conceded
1783 Convention of Volunteers in Dublin
1791 Society of United Irishmen founded
1792–3 Catholic Relief Acts ease penal laws
1795 Orange Order founded
1798 United Irishmen's rising fails
1800 Acts of Union abolish Irish parliament
1803 Robert Emmet's rising fails
1823 Daniel O'Connell forms Catholic Association
1829 Catholic emancipation conceded
1831 National education system established
1840 O'Connell forms National Repeal Association
1842 Thomas Davis founds *The Nation*
1845–9 Potato famine
1848 Young Irelanders' rising fails
1858 Irish Republican Brotherhood founded: beginning of Fenian movement
1867 Fenian rising fails: execution of 'Manchester martyrs'
1870 Isaac Butt forms Home Government Association
1873 Home Rule League formed
1879 Michael Davitt forms Irish National Land League: land war begins
1880 Charles Stewart Parnell leads Irish parliamentary party at Westminster
1881 Gladstone concedes land reform
1882 Parnell released from jail after 'Kilmainham treaty': Lord Frederick Cavendish assassinated in Dublin
1886 Gladstone's first Home Rule Bill defeated
1889 Parnell cited in divorce action
1891 Death of Parnell
1893 Gladstone's second Home Rule Bill defeated: Gaelic League founded
1899 Irish Literary Theatre founded
1904 Abbey Theatre opened
1905 Arthur Griffith founds Sinn Féin movement
1912 Ulster Covenant signed
1913 Formation of Ulster Volunteer Force, Irish Citizen Army and Irish Volunteers
1914 Gun-running by UVF and Irish Volunteers: Government of Ireland Act passed but suspended
1916 Easter Rising in Dublin fails: its leaders are executed
1918 Sinn Féin wins majority of Irish seats at Westminster
1919 First Dáil Éireann meets in Dublin: War of Independence begins
1920 Government of Ireland Act provides for separate parliaments in Northern and Southern Ireland
1921 Truce followed by Anglo-Irish Treaty
1922 Treaty approved by Second Dáil: establishment of Irish Free State followed by Civil War: deaths of Griffith and Michael Collins
1923 Civil War ends
1937 Eamon de Valera introduces new Irish Constitution
1949 Republic of Ireland established

INDEX OF NAMES

Page references in **bold** type refer to the 'lives', and those in *italic* type refer to the illustrations.